THE COACHING
BUSINESS BLUEPRINT

THE COACHING BUSINESS BLUEPRINT

Everything You Need To Start, Run, and Build a Professional Coaching Business

Kay Sanders

KAY SANDERS COACHING

THE COACHING BUSINESS BLUEPRINT

Everything You Need To Start, Run, and Build a Professional Coaching Business

For information address:

Kay Sanders Coaching

www.kaysanders.com

Table of Contents

ACKNOWLEDGEMENT

I would like to thank and acknowledge all those who played a big part in becoming who I am today. Those who taught me about sales, coaching and holistic treatment approaches including Eric Lofholm, John Pyron, John Kuberka, Jamie Engelhardt, and Elisabeth Bouchard.

Most of all I would like to thank my parents, my sister and most of all, my son Darian for being supportive and for standing by my side all this time. Their love and support has inspired me to write this book.

INTRODUCTION

Dear Friend,

For the past few years, I have searched for a comprehensive book on coaching that not only includes coaching topics on different niches, or how to coach, but also the other important parts such as how to grow your business, how to sell and get prospects to hire you as a coach. When I first started the coaching business in 2012 I learned about the niche I wanted to coach in but I did not learn how to actually conduct coaching sessions, nor did I know how to sell my services. So of course I struggled and I was too afraid of finding coaching clients because I was lacking the skills and knowledge about how to actually coach someone. I researched many different books about coaching and sales and even became a Sales Trainer with Eric Lofholm International and I learned all about selling and its process.

The reason for writing this book is because I want to provide a comprehensive blueprint for anyone who is interested in becoming a coach or starting the coaching business but simply doesn't know where to start or how to grow their business. Many who start don't consider all the aspects of a coaching business. It's not only about knowing how to coach someone but also about knowing how to build and grow your business, from having an appealing website, creating your own product, holding workshops, generating leads, generating passive income, and so much more.

Because of my personal experience and having to learn everything from scratch through research and trial and error, I decided to write this book. From working with different people who are starting out as coaches, who are in sales, or who are struggling to get their business off the ground, I found a new mission in my life to not only coach individuals to a more fulfilling life or increase in their sales results, but also to help those who want to become successful in their own coaching business. I know out of experience how difficult it can be trying to start a business. You simply can't think of everything but there are important aspects you simply have to consider and implement in order to become successful.

First of all, I do want to congratulate you for starting your coaching business or even wanting to start a coaching business. Being a coach is one of the best businesses you can start, because you can really make a difference in people's lives and there is nothing better than to see the positive changes people make in their life and finally are able to live the life they truly want and deserve.

Who is this book for? Anyone who wants to either become a coach and simply doesn't know where to get started, or anyone who already started their coaching business but would like extra guidance on growing and building a profitable coaching practice. Even if you are just trying to get an idea of what coaching is, you are still going to benefit from the content of this book because you can use what you are learning to become your own life coach and make changes in your own life.

ABOUT THE AUTHOR

I am a certified Personal Development Coach and Sales Coach, who draws from my own experiences and struggles in life and in sales to inspire others and to make a difference in their lives. I was born and raised in Germany and moved to the U.S. with the desire of achieving big things in life. My passion and dedication to fulfill my life purpose helped me overcome all the roadblocks that kept getting in the way, trying to keep me from accomplishing what I had set out to do. In the process, I found my passion for personal development and success and discovered the way to change my own beliefs, my mindset, and my actions which guided me and allowed me to become the great coach I am today.

I have guided my clients to personal mastery and success. Through teaching and coaching, my clients were able to make major positive changes – both professionally and personally. It is my goal to help people from around the globe who want to live a more fulfilling life or who want to increase their sales results and take their sales career to the next level. I will push them to their limits and build up their confidence to really make things happen.

Through the coaching process I work with clients to clarify their goals and visions, identify key strategic milestone objectives, uncover hidden challenges and blind spots that could be sabotaging their success, and create a long term plan and a next step action plan.

I bring a wide range of experience and education to the table which my clients can benefit from. I have created a Sales Acceleration Training Program that teaches the proper sales process, goal setting, personal growth and self-improvement which will assist individuals in the sales industry to become a sales superstar.

I truly believe that everyone not only deserves but also has the ability to live a fulfilling life full of success and achievements.

PART I – THE INS AND OUTS OF COACHING

INTRODUCTION TO COACHING

Coaching is a growing profession and a tool that more and more successful people are using to help them be their best. The Coaching profession initially started out in the world of professional sports, where trainers trained and helped athletes to discover their own strength in their field and to help them achieve their goals and to become winners. Eventually it went beyond training and fitness, and trainers or coaches realized that their athletes would benefit from coaching in other areas of their life.

In the late 1980s early 1990s, the coaching profession made a shift and more and more individuals became professional coaches in various areas such as business coaching, life coaching, sales coaching, relationship coaching, wellness coaching, just to name a few. In the mid-1990s, people began to realize the true potential coaching has for not only sports and careers but also every aspect of life. Coaching became a very valuable and profitable profession where more and more individuals saw the potential of starting their own coaching business.

Coaching in itself is motivational, inspiring, positive, exciting and action driven where the coach helps the client to reach their fullest potential in life. The fundamental belief a coach holds is that every client already holds their own answers. The coach simply assists in finding the answers the clients hold within themselves to bring them out and turn them into positive action. Coaching is about helping the client find their true wants, desires and dreams and assist them in creating their personal "perfect" life. Every person holds within themselves the power to create their own perfect life, the life they truly want, the career or relationship they truly want. However, sometimes they need help in identifying what their true needs and wants are and require the guidance and support to get where they want to be.

Coaching might sound like an easy task but it is far from being easy. It requires a lot of hard work and commitment from the client but if the client truly wants to change and is ready for the change, the benefits the client will get out of coaching are substantial. Even the coach is required to commit to the client and to work hard to keep the client on track and keep them motivated to keep moving forward. But the best part about coaching someone on reaching their fullest potential is the satisfaction of making a difference in someone's life. Effective coaching enables clients rather than trains them or influences them. Instead, it allows for personal transition and a professional coach never makes assumptions, is judgmental, prescriptive or instructive.

Coaching can be done in many different ways such as face-to-face, by phone, video chatting, email, and through one-on-one or also group coaching. Many coaches choose to conduct their sessions by phone or video chatting because it is more convenient not only for the clients but also for the coach because it does not require being at one specific place. Coaching by phone or video chatting is just much simpler and some clients even prefer this type of session over face-to-face because they feel more comfortable and less vulnerable. Coaching can be very intense where the client has to really dig deep to uncover the things that are holding them back from achieving the things they want in life.

With that said, it is important to understand that coaching is nothing like therapy and a coach must stay away from any things that could be interpreted as therapy. The primary focus during a coaching session is to discuss the clients' future and work on ways for them to achieve their goals where as in therapy the past is what is being discussed and a therapist addresses psychological issues and work through issues that happened in the past. This does not mean that personal issues can't be discussed, because a coach can be more than just a coach, a coach can be a friend, a friendly ear that listens to the client if they need to vent before starting the session. However, it should not turn into a therapy session because coaches, unless they have the proper education in counseling or psychotherapy, are no therapists.

Purpose of a Coach

Individuals hire a coach for many different reasons such as wanting to transition into a different career, finding their soul mate, for a sounding board, for help with their career, to make changes or improvements to their health, to lose weight, or to increase their sales results. There are many different reasons why someone would hire a coach but the main reason really is that they know they could be doing better in their life or careers but they simply either feel stuck or don't know how to get to where they want to be on their own. The coaching profession is steadily growing and expanding in many different areas. Anyone who has the desire to become a coach or is an expert in a certain area has the ability to become a coach. Even someone who isn't an expert in a specific area can become an expert because coaching someone in a specific area doesn't mean that you have to be an expert because all a coach does is guide the client to find their own answers and holds them accountable to achieve their goals and dreams.

Why Someone Would Choose To Become A Coach

This is a very good question and since you purchased this book, ask yourself, why do you want to become a coach or if you are already a coach, why did you become a coach?

The coaching profession definitely has its perks over other professions because it not only benefits clients but also coaches because they can apply the things they learn and be their own coach and transform their own lives just as they can transform the lives of their clients. Coaching can be a very rewarding additional career or even an alternative career to all sorts of different people. Helping others to discover their true desires in life and helping them get there is now a proven method which is causing the increase in popularity for why someone would choose to become a professional coach.

Even though the coaching profession has the potential of earning a substantial amount of money, good coaches never focus entirely on the money; instead they are motivated by making a difference in someone's life and by helping others. Those coaches who solely focus on making money will less likely become professional coaches and also won't stay in business for too long; Clients will pick up on the lack of concern the coach has towards them and walk away to look for a coach that cares more about helping them than about making money.

Another reason for why someone would choose to become a coach is because they like to work with people and help them become their best. Also, they have the desire to do something fulfilling in their lives, and they might want the personal and financial freedom that comes with being an entrepreneur, or their own boss.

The coaching profession allows the flexibility and possibility for earning a substantial income where the coach can choose to work from anywhere in the world. Since coaching does not have to be done face-to-face, the coach is not restricted to one location; they could be on a beach for example and conduct their coaching session. No office, meeting rooms, or staff is required to run a profitable coaching business. All that is required is a phone, a computer, and the drive to make a difference in someone's life. Of course, being self-employed has many advantages over a regular full time job. Being your own boss allows you to choose the hours you work, where you want to work and how much you want to charge.

Challenges To Coaching

Many who start the coaching business unfortunately also quit the business before they even have the chance of becoming successful. What many don't understand is that coaching is an ongoing learning process; only if you learn more and practice, practice, and practice some more will you be able to provide outstanding coaching services. Being a coach, there are endless opportunities to grow your business, from having a good number of coaching clients, to creating your own products, writing a book, being hired by a large corporation to coach their staff, to become a successful speaker such as Tony Robbins for example.

However, all these possibilities take time and effort to put in place or to create. As a coach you have to educate yourself and learn new skills to become the best coach you can be. You also need to know how to sell your services and this is one of the areas coaches fail to educate themselves in because they don't think they are sales people and they don't need to learn how to sell. However, selling skills is what will get you clients, it will help you close the deal and will get you hired.

Another aspect many don't consider is the time and energy it requires to build a profitable coaching business. You not only just coach clients; you also have to do your accounting, your advertising, creating all the documents that are required to run a business. Having a coaching business is just like any other business; it requires front end as well as back end work. One could easily get frustrated with everything that comes with owning your own business and give up because especially if you are still working a full time job, building your coaching business to the point where you can walk away from your full time job is not an easy task to do. It requires many hours of your getting all of your ducks in a row to build your business. But once you reach the point where you can walk away from your job because all of your hard work and dedication has paid off, you will look back and you will be glad you did not give up.

As coaching requires continuous development and learning new skills, it is crucial to realize that mistakes will be made but these mistakes will help you to become a better coach. What many see as mistakes or failures are lessons learned, experience gained and opportunity to turn things around and improve.

SKILLS, ABILITIES AND QUALITIES OF A SUCCESSFUL LIFE COACH

Being a coach requires having specific skills and abilities which are essential in order to be a successful coach. It is not enough to have the ability to inspire people, it also requires the ability to empower and motive clients. If a client doesn't feel motivated he less likely will be able to reach his goals. As a coach you encourage the clients to feel excited about their life ahead, and the endless possibilities they have if they continue moving forward instead of giving up.

Giving Appropriate Feedback

A good coach should be able to give appropriate feedback without upsetting or offending the client. Giving appropriate feedback is a learned skill and if you have not acquired this skill yet, it would be best if you do so. Once you have learned the skill of giving appropriate and supportive feedback, you will be able to empower your clients and energize them towards reaching their goals.

Having Outstanding Communication Skills

As a coach, you are expected to have proper and outstanding communication skills. When you reach out to clients if it's by phone, in person, or even through email, you should be able to reach out to them with a clear message so they understand exactly what you mean. Outstanding communication skills not only require you to give clear, concise messages but also for you to understand, respond and interpret the message you are getting from your clients accordingly and precisely.

Being Creative

A coach should also be creative and if you love what you do and you enjoy working and helping your clients then creativity should be relatively easy. Being able to be creative is a necessity during coaching because it will help you come up with different ways and strategies to help your clients discover more about themselves which then will help you move them towards their goals. To tap into your creativity simply clear your mind of all the clutter and stress that's occupying your mind; meditation is a good way to clear your mind.

Showing Empathy

Being able to show empathy, being compassionate and understanding these are very important skills to have. Only if you truly care about your clients will you be able to help them reach their goals. Put yourself in your clients' shoes to understand where they are coming from, what they are going through and what could be holding them back. Your job as a coach is to understand and emphasize with your clients, show them that they can trust you. Only if they trust you will you be able to help them.

Having Good Observation skills

As a coach you should be able to read your client to get a better understanding of their personality and how they perceive you as a coach. Observe your clients when you speak with them, as this will also help you discover any hidden obstacles or things you could use to coach them on at a later time. Become a detective and study their verbal and nonverbal behavior to determine if your client feels uncomfortable with what you are telling them.

Being positive

As a coach you should have a positive attitude not only when working with clients but also towards life in general. Positivity is contagious and if you as a coach stay positive and have an uplifting mood your clients will pick up on that positivity and become more positive themselves. Also, people would rather surround themselves with positive people than negative people.

COACHING PROCESS AND STRUCTURE

The coaching process has three phases; the first phase is determining and clarifying what the client wants. The second step is mapping out an action plan where you help the client identify key strategic objectives to get what they want and also uncover any hidden challenges that could be holding them back or sabotaging their success, as well as steps to overcome those obstacles and challenges. The third step is all about supporting your client and keeping them motivated to follow through with what they have set out to do and if they lose motivation or get blindsided, getting them back on the right track toward reaching their goals, dreams and desires.

There are two objectives to coaching, one is helping clients by reinforcing the new things they learn and the second is helping them change their behaviors and actions to produce new and better results. In order to provide outstanding coaching, coaches must first learn a lot about themselves before they can coach others. This does not mean that you have to have a perfect life with no problems yourself but you at least should have gone through some things yourself and worked on yourself to discover and overcome a number of personal issues. By working on yourself first it will give you a deeper understanding and it will make your journey of becoming a coach much more meaningful and valuable.

Each coach has a different style of how they coach but every coach should at least follow a certain structure for the coaching session. Having a structure will not only help the coach stay focused and on track but it will also help the client because he or she will know what to expect and it will help them stay focused and on track as well. Every session should be structured the same. For example, if you give homework at the end of the session you should not switch it up where one week you give homework the next one or two sessions you don't. Be consistent and stick to the structure.

When starting out with a client you first need to establish the context for the coaching which includes educating the client what coaching is and what it involves, what they should expect, have they signed the coaching agreement, does the client understand your pricing packages, and any additional information that would help the client get a clear picture of what to expect.

Once the context was established, both the coach and client need to define which area of life the client wants to be coached on and their goals and overall expected outcome. It is important for the coach to know what the clients short and long term goals consist of in order to provide effective coaching sessions. If the coach does not have a clear picture of what the client wants to accomplish or change in their life's the coaching sessions will turn into meaningless conversations instead of pinpointing action steps the client should take to reach their goals.

Each session the coach should review and confirm what was learned and what action steps were taken so far and what action steps need to be taken until the next coaching session. This review and confirming will assist the client and the coach in holding the client accountable. However, if a client fails to complete one or all of the action steps the coach should refrain from making judgments in regards to the speed the client is moving forward. Some clients might take a little longer to accomplish their action steps and it might be more challenging for them than they had anticipated.

As with everything in life, coaching comes to an end eventually. At the end of the coaching assignment, the client should feel that the coaching was worthwhile and definitely had an impact on their life. Sometimes, there might even be room for additional coaching in other areas which would make ongoing support a valuable option to offer to clients. Some clients are open for further coaching at a later time.

THE "HOW TO" OF COACHING

Building rapport with clients

Rapport is defined as mutual trust, being in sync with someone, or being on the same wavelength. Building rapport is probably the most important skill you must have in order to form a sustainable coaching relationship with your clients. In coaching, rapport will reduce resistance and will allow you to connect with your clients on a deeper level. If rapport is not present either from the coach or the client, neither one will get anything out of the session. It doesn't matter how good of a coach you are, if you are not able to build rapport with your clients, the coaching relationship will not last and the client will not open up to you.

Once we have built that connection or rapport with someone, we have a communication style that is harmonious to both individuals. To build rapport with someone, you must learn to control yourself, your breathing, your speech patterns, eye contact, your posture and your use of language. Building rapport can be done in two ways; one is mirroring where you and your client get into alignment and then leading them towards a goal you both agree.

What that means is to build rapport with someone through mirroring you would match their speech patterns. If they speak fast, you speed up your speech rate, if they speak slowly, and you slow down as well. If they sit across from you with their arms or legs crossed, you do the same, if they lean in when they speak, you do the same. You get the point. Once you get into alignment you can lead them into more comfortable behavior for example, slowing down your breathing if needed, sitting more relaxed, and adjusting your speech rate to relax the conversation. Once you notice your client follows your behavior, you now begin to lead the conversation.

Many coaches work with their clients by phone but even if they don't have face-to-face contact, it is still important to build trust and rapport. One way of building rapport by phone is to enter every coaching session or call make with a smile; even though your client can't see your smile, they can hear it in your voice. Adding a little excitement in your voice will let the client know that you are happy to be working with them. If for some reason you still have trouble building that initial rapport you could even talk about the weather or have some small talk for a few minutes before beginning with the session.

Building rapport with a stranger happens as soon as you meet them and it continues to grow. Usually the first thirty seconds are the most important when first meeting someone and during that short time they determine if they like you and if they feel comfortable talking with you. More details about building instant trust and rapport with someone will be discussed in Part III.

If you are not familiar with how to best build rapport, know that it is a skill in which you can learn and improve. There is a simple exercise you can do to practice building rapport. The way we do this is through matching and mismatching what the other person does, or how they behave. To do this exercise you first need to find a willing partner and a quiet place where you won't be interrupted.

The first step is *talking and observing*. Begin the conversation and ask your partner questions to get them talking. Notice their physical posture and gestures as they speak, notice their speech rate. Do they speak fast and loud or slow and soft?

The second step is *increasing rapport by matching*. What that means is continue talking to them and begin to match their posture, their gesture and speech rate. If they are leaning towards you while they speak, lean in too; if they cross their legs, cross yours too. if they speak fast, speed up your speech rate or if they speak slowly then slow down your speech to match theirs. Continue for a few minutes until you notice that you and your partner match well.

The third step is *decreasing rapport by mismatching*. Now that you have increased rapport through matching your partner's behavior you now decrease rapport by starting to deliberately mismatch what your partner is doing. For example, look away, move around more, cross your arms, cross your legs, talk extremely fast or extremely slow, and simply be completely different. Do this until you are sure it had an effect.

After doing this exercise feel free to ask your partner when they noticed that you two were matching or in synch, and what effect the matching and mismatching had on them. You should practice this exercise until you feel comfortable with effectively building rapport. Once you learn this skill, your coaching skills will also increase because you will be more effective with your clients.

Effective Listening

Learning the skills of effective listening will help you as a coach to see the world through the eyes of your clients, which will allow you to have a deeper understanding and enhance your capacity for empathy for your client which is an essential part of your coaching relationships with your clients. Most people don't really listen, or they only listen with one ear which leads to misunderstandings and miscommunications. Have you ever had a conversation with someone where you could really feel that this person truly heard you? Unfortunately this phenomenon does not happen very often because our minds are preoccupied with our own problems and thoughts, which doesn't allow us to really focus on the person to whom we are speaking or "listening".

As a coach however, active listening is a must have and is also one of the Core Competencies the ICF (International Coaching Federation) defines for coaching. The ICF defines active listening as *"the ability to focus completely on what the client is saying and is not saying, to understand the meaning of what is said in the context of the client's desires, and to support client self-expression"*

Active listening requires a great degree of sensitivity and the coach must not only understand what the client is saying but also what they feel. The coach must pay close attention to the client and then repeat what the client said in their own words as well as what he or she thinks the client said and feels. The coach doesn't not have to agree what the client said but he or she must simply understand and state what they think the client said. By repeating what the client said, the client can clarify in case the coach misunderstood what they said or rephrase what they said. Active listening forces the coach to listen attentively which will avoid any misunderstandings. It also tends to help clients open up and to get them to say more.

In order to actively listen to clients, the coach must clear his or her mind and empty themselves of any personal concerns, troubles or distractions as well as any preconceptions they might have, prior to the coaching session. Meditating prior to the coaching session will help to ground yourself and to put all personal thoughts aside, and will allow you to fully focus and concentrate on the client.

Active listening as a coach not only pertains to listening to the client but also becoming self-aware and recognizing any thoughts and reactions that may come up, and to put those aside to prevent such thoughts to influence the overall understanding of what the client is saying, feeling, or is not saying. By being self-aware as a coach, and actively listening to one's own thoughts and reactions to the client, one demonstrates authenticity.

There are different active listening techniques a coach can apply which will assist in truly understanding their clients. One technique is paraphrasing where the coach restates in their own words what the client said. This allows for testing the understanding of what the client meant as well as letting them know that the coach actively listens to them.

The second technique is reflection, which is slightly different from paraphrasing because the coach tells the client what they believe the client feels rather than what they said. This is particularly helpful when the client expresses strong feeling.

The third technique is the neutral technique, where the coach encourages the client to continue talking. The coach simply nods their head or says something like "uh-huh". By doing so, it tells the client that the coach is listening interested.

The fourth technique is clarifying; the coach would use this technique to get more information about a specific topic and usually by asking additional questions. The firth technique is summarization and involves the coach combining the client's thoughts into statements by focusing on the clients key points.

Asking questions

As a coach it is important to ask open-ended questions, questions that will stimulate the client's emotion and inspire creativity to aid in their coming up with their own answers to problems. Asking clients the right questions will help you understand them better on a deeper level and then use that knowledge to guide them on their way of personal development and to reaching their goals and desires. Coaches are considered leaders in creating powerful questions to evoke transformations and inspire their clients. Asking the right questions is just as important as actively listening because only if you listen actively will you be able to form powerful open-ended questions which will allow the client to not only open up more but also to discover things they may have never considered.

Most people don't ask the right questions or they ask closed-ended questions which don't allow for a lot of elaboration or deep thoughts so conversations seem rather shallow. Asking the right types of questions are crucial to the outcome and results we coaches aim to achieve with our clients. Know this, asking open-ended question is a learned skill, just as actively listening, and if you are not good in asking the right questions, you can learn and improve your skills which will help you in becoming a great coach. Ask yourself these questions, when you listen to your clients what are you really listening for? How do you ask questions and how can you achieve a greater impact with the questions you ask?

The purpose of asking effective and open-ended questions is for the coach to gain clarity, a better understanding, and perspective of the client. It provokes deeper or alternative thinking by the client; it will also help in challenging their current thinking and beliefs. It will help clients in evaluating themselves and their situation and it will help in exploring different options, facts, thoughts, and feelings. It also allows the client to look at their problems from a different point of view so they can plan and take action accordingly.

Good questions are simple. They have a purpose and they are influencing without being controlling and most of all, they are questions the client is willing to answer. A good coach tries to keep a balance between being influencing and controlling. If the coach asks controlling questions the client might feel pushed and it could come across as the coach being judgmental towards the client and it can damage the rapport between coach and client and also can damage the ongoing relationship. As a coach it is also important to avoid making the client feel wrong about what they said or what they did because it also can damage the relationship.

Before asking the client any questions, ask yourself the same question to identify if the question you are about to ask is appropriate or if it may be offending, judgmental, or simply just a wrong question to ask. Sometimes we blurt out whatever question comes to mind and those questions might seem appropriate but when looking at the questions more closely, we might discover that we should either rephrase them or not ask them at all.

In the end, asking the right questions is a process and only with practice will you become better. But keep in mind, questions are building blocks that you can build on and learn from and will aid you in becoming more creative with your clients and most of all a successful coach.

Let's take a look at some open-ended questions a coach can ask their clients.

1. What do you want in life?

2. What is your purpose?

3. How will it feel when you reach your goal?

4. What does that look like?

5. What is getting in the way of living the life you truly want?

6. If you could live the life you truly want, what changes would you have to make to get there?

7. What areas of your life could be adjusted or could use some changes?

8. What are three things you would want to change over the next six months?

9. Imagine how it would feel like once you accomplished this.

10. What do you really, really want?

11. What are you currently accepting or putting up with in your life?

12. What is one thing or area in your life that you could change that would bring you more peace/freedom/happiness?

13. What do you need to do to get there?

14. If you could do one thing every day, something that excites you to get out of bed every day, what would that be?

15. What is stopping you?

16. What research could you do to help you determine what steps you need to take to accomplish _____?

17. What are three action steps you could take right now or within the next week/month that would get you one step closer to _____?

18. On a scale of 1-10 how do you feel about taking these action steps?

19. What would need to happen to increase that commitment level?

20. What will happen or what is the cost of your not doing this?

21. What excites you and makes you feel alive?

22. What makes you smile? How can you add more of that to your day/life?

23. Let's set a deadline, by when do you want to accomplish this?

24. How have you changed from where you were a child/teen/young adult?

25. If you were to paint a picture of your life six months/one year from now, what would that look like?

26. What can you learn from this?

27. In what way is the current situation extremely bad/perfect?

28. If you were your own coach, what would you tell yourself right now?

29. What can you feel grateful for in your current situation?

30. Imagine you were 90, what would you like to say about yourself and what life story would you like to be able to tell?

31. If you could do anything and knew you could not fail, what would you do? Why?

32. Who do you admire?

33. Who would you have to become to be the person you want to be?

34. About what are you passionate?

35. What is your greatest strength? How can you bring more of that to your current/future career/life/relationships?

36. What are you passionate about? What excites you?

37. Of what are you afraid?

38. Who can you talk to in order to get more clarity about
    _____?

39. In what areas do you need more clarity or improvement?

40. What are some of your weaknesses?

41. If your life/health/relationship would be ideal – what is one thing that would be different?

42. Is money or job satisfaction more important to you?

43. Can you tell me more?

44. What opportunities do you have?

45. What are some of the challenges you have?

46. How does this fit with your plans/goals?

47. If you could do it all over again would you do it differently? How? Why?

48. What is stopping you from reaching your financial goal?

49. What does success mean to you?

50. Are you ready to make a commitment?

As you can see all these questions are open-ended and require a more elaborated answer than just a yes or a no type of answer. These questions are meant to make the client think about the answer and they have to dig deep to honestly answer these questions. Don't be afraid of looking silly by asking a lot of questions. Instead, focus on the outcome and on your initiative of asking questions in the first place. Your clients will feel like you truly care because you are trying to find out more about them and about what is going on in their life. If you don't ask questions, you will not be able to help your clients because you won't know what they want, why they want it, and what is holding them back from getting what they want.

Giving Feedback

As mentioned earlier, a coach must be able to give appropriate feedback to their clients to be supportive but not offending. Throughout the coaching relationship, clients are able to experience a different view of themselves as well as their situation. As a coach, being able to give effective feedback can accelerate a client's learning, inspire and motivate them to take action. To maintain a positive attitude a coach must learn to give feedback with positive intention, based on facts or the client's behavior, and most of all it must be beneficial to the client. A coach must know when it is a good time to give feedback. They can do this in two ways. One is through mirroring back what the client said, to allow clarification on what was said; two is the coach providing an observation. Even though there are no specific rules as to when to give feedback a coach should only offer feedback when he feels the client would benefit from it.

Sometimes it is necessary for the coach to give feedback if the client for example has not noticed something. They might be stuck in their process or thought or they might avoid something that would be of benefit to them. These are areas where a client would benefit from receiving feedback but clients sometimes also ask to receive feedback. In the case the client asks to receive feedback but the coach feels uncomfortable giving feedback, avoid giving feedback that will make the client feel uncomfortable. Instead, the coach could ask the client what they feel is not working and have a discussion about what is going on. However, the coach should not give inappropriate feedback or be controlling, but encouraging and challenging them towards success.

Giving feedback can sometimes be a bit challenging especially if it is negative feedback. However, if the feedback causes a negative response from the client, the coach should apologize for causing their response. If it is not clear why the client got upset the coach could simply ask for clarification: "I think I may have upset you with what I have said – am I correct?" By asking for clarification the coach then can rephrase or explain what they have said. Situations like this will give the coach the opportunity to learn from their experience which will assist in their growth.

Giving appropriate feedback is a learned skill and while you learn how to effectively give feedback be advised that you will make mistakes. However, it is up to you to learn from your mistakes and to focus on improving your skills.

Beliefs

Our beliefs are formed by what we learned from our parents and what we have learned through personal experiences. They even include things we have learned from others, and those beliefs become part of our identity. They can either help us move forward, or they can hold us back from seeing and fulfilling our true potential. We all have our own concept of the world. Your concept of the world, for example, is different from mine, but we all know how we see things and the way we feel about things. Every day we are being influenced by different entities, such as the media, friends, family, and even coworkers or strangers you meet in a coffee shop. We form our beliefs from what influences us, but it is up to each one of us to decide what beliefs we keep and what beliefs we allow to influence our every move. Our strongly held beliefs drive us to take action, and you have to choose the beliefs that challenge you and move you forward instead of holding you back.

All beliefs whether they are positive or negative exist for a reason. Some act as comfortable protective armor because they protect us from getting hurt. For example, let's say you have always had bad luck regarding relationships. Every guy you have met cheated on you, always lied to you, and maybe even treated you badly. Because of those experiences, you developed a negative mind-set concerning relationships and it might be something like the following: "Every guy I meet turns out to be a loser. They all lie and cheat on me. No guy ever treats me right."

Such thinking will keep you from ever meeting the right guy because you have already decided that the next guy you meet will be just like all these other guys. Even though such negative thinking will sabotage you from meeting the guy of your dreams, it also acts as a protective barrier because you already expect that something bad will happen. Accordingly, you won't allow yourself to let your guard down because the guy might not be the type of guy you expect. All these negative thoughts or beliefs take root on a subconscious level, and most people use limiting beliefs because it keeps them safe in their comfort zone. We have all done it!

Our actions today are influenced by interpretations we have made in the past, both positive and negative. Our most limiting beliefs about ourselves may get in the way of any actions we need to take to move forward and accomplish what we want to achieve. If we believe we are not smart enough to get that job we want so badly or that we are not pretty enough to meet our soul mate, then we basically give ourselves permission to not even try. If we believe that all men or women we meet or date are cheaters, liars, and simply no good, we will end up building that protective barrier around ourselves to protect us from getting hurt. Such limits may protect us, but in reality they are very limiting because they keep us from ever being in a happy relationship.

Anthony Robbins said: "Beliefs have the power to create and the power to destroy."

Our beliefs are what determine our life and the things we want. They create that reality. Who we are is based on our beliefs, and they determine our behavior, our feelings, and our thoughts.

Have you ever wondered why the things you wish for simply don't come true? Have you wished for a better job or to meet Mr. or Mrs. Right, but instead you are still stuck with a job you are not very happy with and every guy or female you meet turns out to be far from what you wanted? Does this sound familiar? One possible explanation for this problem could be that your mind-set is getting in the way of your getting the things you want in just the way you want them. The mind is a very powerful tool that can either push or guide us to become successful or hold us back.

I had never really thought about how much my mind could affect my life until a few years ago when I was reading the book *You Become What You Think About* by Vic Johnson. It was really an eye-opener since it became clear to me how much I had been hurting myself because of my negative and limiting mind-set. After reading this book, I did some soul searching and discovered the origin of some of my limiting beliefs and how they had been affecting my life.

When I first started in network marketing many years ago, I always thought "they are not going to spend their hard-earned money on this!" And that's exactly what had happened. I became quite frustrated because I never was able to make a sale. Even though at first I thought it was because of the products in fact it was my mind-set that was holding me back because I always felt pushy and uncomfortable asking for the money.

Being in sales, however, was not the only area of my life that was affected by my limiting mind-set. Other areas, such as my health and relationships, were affected as well. It took me many years to realize that all this time I was sabotaging myself, causing me to be unhappy and miserable. Once I learned about the Law of Belief, my life turned around, and I became much happier. I finally started attracting the things I wanted, and I was able to achieve one goal after another.

The Law of Belief

The Law of Belief is best explained by the following: "What we believe becomes reality." Once we change the way we think about how we act and the world around us, we can change our reality and also our own performance. The Law of Belief is the key to happiness and success. Once we truly believe that we can become successful and accomplish what we want or have anything we want, we will have it in just that way. But if we don't truly believe, then we hold ourselves back and don't achieve what we want to achieve.

"It is not until you believe it that you will see it."

How many times have you wanted something, but it simply did not happen for you? It is our limiting beliefs that keep us from getting the things we want in just the way we want them. You may want to have something or have it in a certain way, but deep down you don't truly believe that you can attain it.

Henry Ford once said: "Whether you think you can or whether you think you can't, you're right."

In order for the Law of Belief to be effective, you must first know exactly what it is that you want in exactly the way you want it. Once you have a crystal-clear picture of what you want and truly believe that you can and will have it in just that way, you will slowly but surely manifest the things you truly want. But you must believe!

Many who try to apply the Law of Belief fail or give up too soon because just like everything else in life things take time to happen? If you don't continually reinforce your beliefs, you might end up giving up too soon. Being consistent and maintaining focus on your goals is possibly the greatest challenge you have to face. You have to maintain your faith and belief that things will change and that you will accomplish what you have set out to do even though setbacks and roadblocks are trying to prevent you from accomplishing your goals.

The path to success and happiness is not always easy, but even obstacles can be seen as something positive because we can learn from our setbacks, and they allow us to grow as a person. If you look back and think about all the obstacles you have had to face throughout your life, were they all truly bad, or did you learn from them, and did they help you make better choices the next time you faced the same obstacle?

Such obstacles make us who we are today. They help us grow as a person, and they guide us to make better decisions later in life. I believe that everything happens for a reason and that no matter what we have to go through in life, we all have a choice to continue moving forward or giving up at the first sign of trouble. If we choose to give up, we can never hope to reach our goals, but once we learn to persevere, we eventually create the reality we truly deserve.

In order to make the Law of Belief work in your favor, you must begin to believe. You must clearly understand what it is that you want to achieve and then decide what you have to do to accomplish your goals. You need to get into the habit of acting as if you had already accomplished these goals.

Our behavior influences our beliefs, and it helps manifest our desire, and all personal breakthroughs begin with a change in beliefs.

The Subconscious Mind

The way our mind works is pretty simple. It consists of two parts: the conscious mind and the subconscious mind. Think of it as an iceberg where the top 10 percent that you see above the water is your conscious mind. The other 90 percent of the iceberg that's beneath the water, the part you can't see, is your subconscious mind. So which part do you think really drives our behavior? The subconscious mind. We all have certain beliefs about ourselves on a subconscious level that prevent us from achieving our potential. Any negative beliefs you have about yourself or your abilities act as an anchor that is holding you back from achieving certain things in life.

Our actions are controlled by our subconscious mind, and if our conscious mind is not in harmony with our belief system or our subconscious mind, our actions will not produce any results. The purpose of the subconscious mind is to keep us consistent with our identity and how we describe ourselves to others.

"We become what we say. We become our self image, matching to our self-belief."

Negative/Limiting Beliefs

The mind is a very interesting entity and easily influenced. Did you know that we hurt ourselves just by our thoughts? Have you ever had a situation where on a subconscious level, not knowing that you are doing it, you talk yourself into having the worse pain ever or where you talk yourself into being too afraid of something that you decide not to do it after all? Our brain believes what we tell it. If we think pain, we get pain; if we think fear, we get fear. The root cause of limiting beliefs stems from a fear of failure or fear of rejection. You might wish for a better position where you are employed, but deep down you might fear that you won't live up to the expectations that come with the position. This type of limiting belief was formed with positive intentions to protect you from the pain that would come from failure and not being able to live up to expectations and perhaps even being fired. All our mind is trying to do is protect us from the pain and agony that come with failure, disappointment, or rejection.

Everything starts with a thought, and if we think bad thoughts, bad things happen, but if we think good thoughts, good things happen.

"Things only have the meaning that we give them."

Positive Self Talk—Affirmations

We have around 50,000 thoughts every day, and 95 percent of these are repeated daily. One way to reprogram the subconscious mind is through autosuggestion, which means that you repeat to yourself the same thing over and over and over again. Change begins with language, and there is a vocabulary to success.

Affirmations are a powerful tool that you can use to reprogram your subconscious mind and influence your life. Affirmations are positive statements that are repeated out loud to change your beliefs, habits, and thought patterns. Through repetition, the subconscious mind accepts the affirmation, and the statement becomes part of your way of thinking. The subconscious mind is the root of our issues; if you have limiting beliefs, they are embedded deep in your subconscious mind. By using affirmation frames, you can free your subconscious mind and eliminate these beliefs.

Through affirmation frames, you can achieve excellence through motivation. You will approach your life with a passion, drive, energy, and motivation to make the most of everything and achieve success. You are able to increase your desires and level of ambition to fuel your motivation instead of settling for second best. You will be able to take more action instead of procrastinating. And most of all, you will be able to change the way your mind works and start enjoying getting things done and the reward that comes with being highly motivated.

A positive affirmation is simply a statement that affirms something is true. Through repetition and consistency, the statement becomes stored in your mind and starts changing your beliefs. It influences your personality and even alters your behavior. For example, if you say such phrases as "I can do anything I put my mind to" or "I am a master in sales" and say such phrases over and over and over again, eventually you will start to really believe it, and it will influence your personality. Most of all, you will become more confident.

Consistency is the key to using affirmation to change your way of thinking. As you know, change doesn't happen overnight, and even though affirmation frames are very powerful, they do take time to have a positive effect. Make a commitment to recite your affirmations every day three times a day—best to do this in the morning, during the day, and in the evening. Say your affirmations out loud ten times each day and you will quickly notice a difference. You could even record yourself saying the affirmations and listen to it three times a day or at night. If the noise doesn't bother you, you could let the recording play throughout the night.

"Change begins in language, and when you change your language, you can change your reality."

I am about to share with you some affirmation phrases that I use myself and that you can use if you feel you are holding yourself back because you fear failure.

 ➢ I will achieve great things
 ➢ I am capable of massive success

- I stay positive at all times
- I stay persistent until I achieve success
- I persist despite any setbacks
- I go all out to achieve my goals
- Nothing is stopping me from accomplishing my goals
- I put full effort into any tasks I start
- Success comes naturally to me
- I always pursue my dreams
- I will achieve my ultimate potential in life
- I only think positively about myself and my ambitions
- I make a difference in the world
- I have everything I need to become successful

Just as positive affirmations change our behavior and beliefs, negative thoughts or limiting beliefs do the same. Examples of such limiting beliefs could be that "I'm not experienced enough," "I'm not good enough," "I don't have it in me," "I don't have a college degree," "I'm too old," "I don't have any money," "I'm too afraid," "I don't have the time." If we focus on such limiting beliefs, they will end up holding us back because our subconscious mind adapts to what we say to ourselves, which results in holding ourselves back and limiting ourselves from accomplishing great things.

Affirmation, Visualization, and The Law of Attraction go hand in hand because the way we think or the things we think about also applies to the things we have in life. We attract the things we focus on the most. Unfortunately, most people focus on what they don't want instead of focusing on the things they do want. For example, if you want to become successful with your business or your sales career, focus on that. See it as if it has already happened. Feel how it will feel when you are successful. The same thing applies if you are currently renting and your dream is to own your own home. Draw a mental picture of having that—your dream home. Picture it exactly the way you want it.

By focusing on what you want, you basically think it into existence—your subconscious mind always catches up with what we think about, so if you think big, you will get big. If you think successful, you will become successful, but if you keep focusing on negative things and think you will never be able to make it in sales or that you will never be able to own your dream home, guess what's going to happen—nothing! Nothing is going to happen because you don't allow yourself to let it happen.

Having the proper mind-set where your beliefs are in sync with your conscious mind is especially important and affects many different aspects in life, including happiness, success, relationships, career, health, and even finances. If you truly want to live a more fulfilling life and accomplish anything you want, you must change your mind-set and truly believe in yourself and that you deserve to have whatever it is you desire in just the way you want it. Doing this is the key to lifelong success and happiness.

This not only pertains to you but also your clients, your clients too have limiting beliefs and sabotaging their own success, it is up to you to guide them on their way of realizing and identifying those negative beliefs and help them shift their mindset to adopt a positive mindset. You can introduce them to positive affirmations and the Law of Attraction and the Law of Belief.

The Wheel of life

Life can get busy and we start focusing our energy on only one or a few areas of our lives rather than focusing on all areas of our life. Even though focusing all of your energy on a specific project or area is beneficial to get things done, if you take it too far, you can be frustrated or stressed, leading to, health issues, insomnia, fatigue and other issues. When you notice that you have been spending more time focusing on one area and completely ignoring other areas in your life, it is time to take a closer look of your overall life in order to bring your life back into balance.

The Wheel of Life can help and is commonly used by coaches in defining areas in client's life that are out of balance to provide a stress-free life.

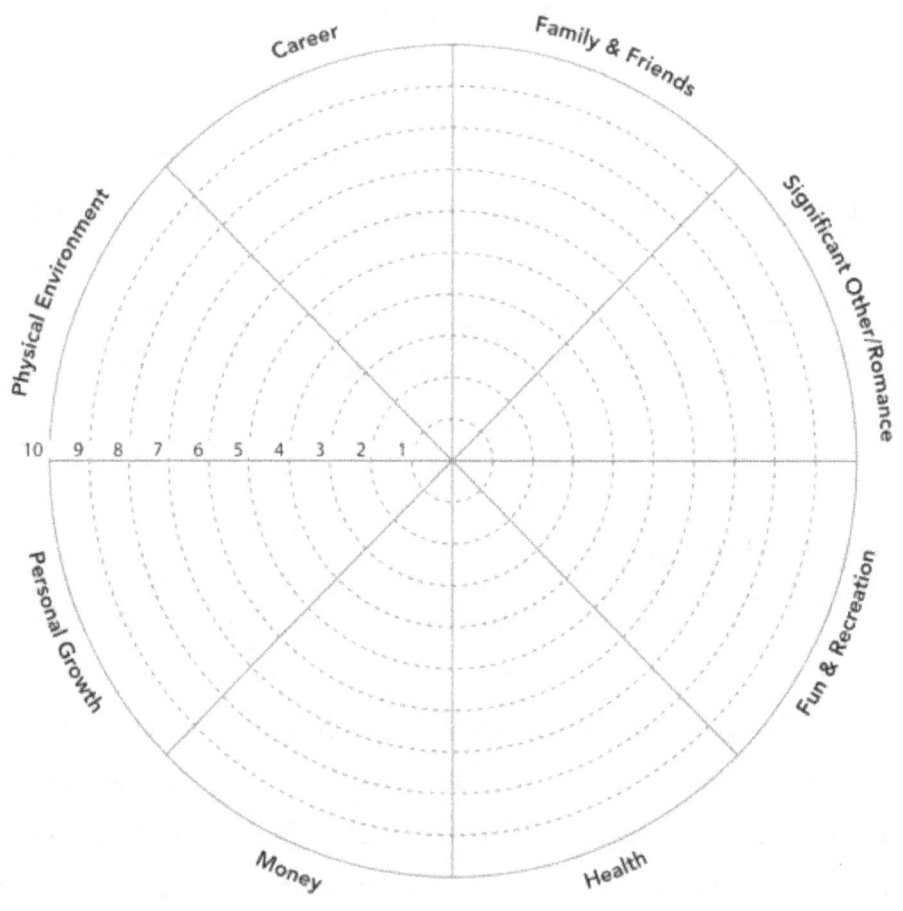

The wheel of life is commonly used by coaches because it helps create a foundation for goal setting. It gives a visual presentation of how a person's life is at the moment, instead of how a person would like it to be. Essentially the wheel of life is divided into different categories which are important to a person's life; the image above is an example of most areas of life.

The way to use this tool is by brainstorming each area of your life, considering the role you play, areas that are important to you, and reflecting on the things that are priorities in your life. You simply rate your satisfaction levels from one to ten where one is closest to the center and least satisfying and ten is most satisfying. Simply placing a mark on the line in each area and connecting the marks will give a very good picture of how balanced your life really is and what needs improvement to balance your life.

COACHING MODELS

In coaching, you should be familiar with the two models of coaching. The first model is the enrollment process, considered the initial or complimentary coaching session. The second model is the coaching session format. Both models are required in the coaching process because the enrollment model will help you get clients and the coaching model will help you conduct effective coaching sessions.

There are different things you should consider when coaching someone. First, do they want coaching? If they don't really want to make a change or be coached then it wouldn't matter how good of a coach you are. The client would be less likely to take any action to make a change. You also want to know what the client expects to get out of coaching and from you as their coach. You should also take notes during each session so you won't forget anything because if you coach with multiple clients you quickly can mix up things or even forget what they tell you. This will show the client that you truly care about helping them.

The Enrollment Strategy

The intention of the enrollment strategy is to help you get a better understanding about the prospect's thought process about coaching as well as to decide if they are the right match for your coaching services. Not every person is a good fit for coaching and during the enrollment process you can weed out those who are serious about making a change in their life and those who say they want to change but in all honesty they are not very motivated to put in the work and you would waste your time trying to get them to change. You want to find them "A" clients because those are the ones who will truly benefit from your coaching and you will have the most success and feeling of accomplishment. During the enrollment session or complimentary coaching session you would ask a series of questions to qualify them to find out their true need for coaching and also their commitment level.

Most coaches don't feel comfortable about "selling" their services but in order to fill your coaching practice you have to go out and sell your services. In Part III you will learn the best ways of selling your services that not only provides value to prospects but will also enroll prospects as paying clients.

To give you a better understanding about the enrollment session, the number one priority of all coaching is taking action and motivating prospects to take action and to hire you. You want to show prospects that your coaching service is the solution to their problem and your job as the coach is to uncover their desire to wanting to make a change. You want them to see how you can help them achieve whatever it is they want to achieve, as long as it is in your scope of coaching. The purpose is to help individuals to wanting to make a change and to awaken their desire and to bring clarity to what is going on below the surface. During the enrollment session the prospect will begin to understand what they truly want and to discover some of the things that are holding them back.

When conducting the enrollment sessions you must consider the following process of starting out with building trust and rapport. Next you want to use an agenda script; this will let the prospect know what to expect during and at the end of the session.

"Hello Mr. Prospect this is Kay your coach. (do some small talk to build rapport) *Are you ready for our coaching session?*

"Before we begin, do you mind if I spend a few minutes going over how I usually conduct these sessions?

"Great, first I would like to share with you a little bit about the coaching profession, my specialties and answer any questions you might have. Next I will ask you a series of questions to get a better understanding about your current situation and how to best help you. At the end of our session if we both feel like we are a fit, I will share with you how my ongoing coaching program work, and we then can decide together if it would be of benefit to you to hire me as your coach. How does that sound so far?"

By explaining how you conduct these sessions and also mentioning that you will be talking about your coaching services at the end you already prepare the prospect that you will be asking for the order at the end. By doing the agenda script and letting the prospect know that you will close at the end, they won't be surprised when you start talking about your coaching fees.

The next part would be asking the prospect probing questions to identify their needs for coaching.

"For me to best help you, do you mind if I ask you a few questions and take some notes?" (here are a few sample probing questions you could ask)

- *Are you familiar with what coaching is?* (if they say no, explain what coaching is)

- *Have you ever worked with a coach before?* (this will give you an idea of their level of familiarity about coaching and also could benefit you if they did receive coaching before and saw positive results)

- *What do you expect to get out of coaching?* (this question will help you define what they expect to get out of coaching with you if they would hire you)

- *What is your biggest concern?* (if they are unfamiliar with coaching they might be concerned if coaching is really worth their money and if they had coaching before but bad experience if will help you with demonstrating that not all coaching is bad)

- *What caused you to be interested in this complimentary coaching session?*

- *How do you think would coaching impact your life/business/health* (or whatever else you are coaching on)? (this will give you the stepping stone as to how you could best help them)

Also you should mention that everything discussed will be completely confidential. It would also help to mention the difference between coaching and therapy and that coaching has nothing to do with counseling or therapy. Some people might not know the difference.

The next step is identifying their goals and vision by asking a series of question to find out what their true need and wants are. You could ask something like the following:

- *"If you could have and do anything you would want, where would you like your life/business/health/relationship etc, be within 6 month/a year?"*

- *"If you could have it in just the way you want it, what would that do for you? How would that make you feel?"*

- *"What would be the best part about having it in just that way?"*

You could also use the word "imagine" to have a deeper effect because letting them imagine how their life would be different if they have accomplished what they want to accomplish and their life is just the way they want it will increase the desire to actually make that change and to reach that goal.

Once you defined their goals and raised their desire for really wanting it, you ask them what steps they would have to take to get there; this will give them a plan or an idea of what needs to happen to reach that goal.

Next you help them uncover any challenges that would get in the way or that are holding them back. You could ask questions like:

- *"What do you think is slowing you down or holding you back from having _____ (mention the goals they listed)?"*

- *"What impact do these challenges have on your life/business/health/relationship etc?"*

- *"Can you think of anything else that is standing in your way"?*

Next you motivate them by allowing them to see that there is hope and that they still can achieve what they want. You could do so by asking them how it would feel or what it would do for them if they could turn things around and eliminate the things that are holding them back from reaching their goals. Really connect them with the possibility of reaching their goals and living a more fulfilling life or becoming successful in their business or whatever area they want to improve in.

It is important for you to raise their desire for wanting to change and providing them with the possibility of truly making this happen. Do not try to solve their problem during the enrollment session because if you solve their problem they won't need to hire you, because you already gave them the answer for free. This can be difficult at times especially if you are passionate about helping others. Remember, if you want to grow your business and have clients for longer than just the initial session, avoid solving their problems until they became paying clients.

The next step is sharing the benefits they get from hiring you as their coach. Explain to them how you help people reach their goals; thinking about the way you coach, for example:

"I use a four-step process when coaching my clients. The first step is we get clear about what they truly want and we get crystal clear on their goals because in order to make a change you must be crystal clear about what it is you want. Next we will discover any obstacles that get in the way of reaching your goals. Then we will put in place action steps for you to reach your goals. Last but not least I as your coach will hold you accountable and I will motivate you to keep moving forward."

Next you want to move into the close. You do a quick review of what their challenges are and mention that you have a program specially designed for people with similar challenges and if they would like to hear more about your ongoing coaching program. By asking permission to share with them your coaching services they won't feel like you are pushing them into hiring them. Make it clear that it is totally up to them and that there won't be any hard feelings if they decide not to hire you. Remember it is all about providing value.

If they agree to hear more about your coaching services you would go over your coaching packages, what they get and also the price for each package if you have different packages. Don't rush through this step because if you talk too fast and rush through it the prospect might not get everything you say. You would also cover any special discounts, satisfaction guarantees, how often you would coach them, how long the sessions usually last, if the sessions are done over the phone or face-to-face, and anything else about your coaching program. Then you ask what package would best fit their needs.

You can also make a suggestion right before asking that question in case you have different package deals but don't just pick the highest price package, really think about which package would best fit their needs this will show the prospect that you are choosing in their best interest. When they tell you which package would best fit their needs you simply move into the final close where you ask what credit card they would like to use or if you use PayPal to bill them you ask them for their PayPal email address. The only thing left now is to set up your next coaching session or sessions.

If the prospect gives you objections and doesn't want to make a buying decision at this time you would simply handle the objections in which you will learn about in Part III under Objection Handling.

The Coaching Session

During the coaching session you will be able to get to know your client on a deeper level. They will be sharing their thoughts, struggles, fears, and beliefs which can get very emotional at times but that is a good thing because if the client really opens up to you then you will truly be able to help them because they have trust in you. From the first session on you must identify what your client wants and sometimes it might be a little tricky to find out what they truly want because they might not even know what they really want deep down. However, with a series of question you can uncover what they truly want and take it from there.

Be advised, your clients' goals may change from one session to the next. They might have a change of heart and instead of wanting to work on that one area in their life, they want to work on something completely different because they realized what they thought their goal was truly wasn't all that important to them. In that case, be patient with your client and they might want to work on that one area at a later time or maybe not at all but that is OK. During the session it is all about the client; it doesn't matter what you as the coach wants for them or what you think might be best for them. The session is 100% about the client. Always remember that.

The main goal during each coaching session is to discover their goals that they want to work on for the upcoming week, targeted goals that will help them get one step closer to reaching their targeted goal. You would also discuss any obstacles that could keep them from accomplishing each goal and any action steps they can take to overcome those challenges. Next you also want to define their commitment level for each goal and at the end you would ask them about their overall commitment level to really take action and to make things happen.

If their commitment level is below a seven than you might want to help them either identify why their commitment level is that low and maybe even define different goals which are more important to them and has a higher commitment level. The reason for asking for their commitment level is because if they are not fully committed to completing the goals they set for the upcoming week then they really don't want to accomplish those goals.

Each session, before defining the goals for the upcoming week you would discuss the goals they had set in the previous session and if they were able to accomplish those goals and if not, what was getting in the way and what did they do to try to overcome those challenges. You should also find out if anything changed in regards to their overall goal because things may have come up and the initial goal is no longer important to them.

Sometimes you might have trouble getting your clients to commit to any goals and if that happens, you could take them back to the beginning and reconnect their desire to their overall goal. Always ask a lot of questions to help your clients come up with their own answer. Refrain from giving advice; a coach never gives advice and even if the client asks you for your advice rephrase it so it is a question rather than giving advice. The reason for why coaches do not give advice is because if your client takes your advice to heart and it does not end up the way they wanted it or it had some negative consequences your client will come to you and blame you for their mistake. Instead of giving advice you could do some brainstorming with your clients, where both of you come up with ideas but at the end let your client pick the one that best fits their needs.

During each session you should also give your client homework to complete not only the goals they set out to do but also research on certain topics that could help them achieve their goals, or they could be making a list of certain things, or anything that you can think of that would benefit your client and keeps them motivated. The reason for giving homework is to encourage ongoing learning and motivation to move forward. You could also provide your client with a list of resources that can help them get more information about specific topics that can aid them in reaching their goals. For example if you have a client that wants to lose weight, you could provide a list with resources for healthy eating, or work out exercises. That way you don't have to know all the answers and it motivates the client to do their own research.

***

Now that you have a better understanding of the two coaching models I encourage you to try them out for yourself and tweak them to fit your niche and your style of coaching. If you are just starting out in coaching, this will give you with the proper guidance. One thing I want you to remember is the only way you will become a good coach is to practice consistently and constantly. There will always be instances where you get stuck and might not know what to do but with practice things will get easier and you will become more effective. At least you have something to go by instead of going out there blind not know how to conduct a coaching session and how to enroll prospects into your coaching program. Good luck and enjoy practicing. You will be amazed how powerful some sessions can be and how satisfying it is to hear your clients talk about their wins and accomplishments.

PART II – THE INS AND OUT OF BUILDING A PROFITABLE COACHING BUSINESS

BEFORE GETTING STARTED

Now that you are clear about the coaching process and the "how to" of coaching your next step is learning about how to build a profitable coaching business. It is not enough to know how to coach and to be an effective coach, but there is also the back end of growing your business which includes marketing, advertising and ways to get clients.

Identifying Your Business Dream

The first step in building a profitable coaching business is to identify your dream. As you know and you probably already do this with your clients, is to have them get crystal clear on their dream because only when you know exactly what you want and how you want it, will you be able to achieve and get the things you want. It is important for you to define how you want your business to look like including number of clients, location of the office, number of days you want to coach, etc. Basically you have to pinpoint every little detail about how you want your business, as specifically as you can.

When thinking about how you want your business to be, keep in mind not to dream too big and also not too small; stay in the middle because if you dream too big you might set your expectations too high and don't really have the intention or desire to take the necessary actions to achieve your dreams. If you dream too small, you might end up settling for less than what you really want and what you are capable of achieving.

Also avoid focusing on the things you feel you should have or do in your business, or worry about how you are going to accomplish it. When you work on defining your dreams don't worry about the "how" but instead focus on what you really want because the "how" will come later. You simply take it one step at a time. By focusing on the "how" you might sell yourself short because you might not know "now" how to do it but maybe in the near future you will learn. Just remember this, if you are determined to build a successful and profitable coaching business nothing can keep you from accomplishing what you want. Anything is possible.

To clarify your business dream consider these questions, and write down your answers and review your dreams from time to time to remind you of what it is you want for your business.

- What does your coaching business look like? List anything from coaching individual clients, group coaching, coaching by phone or video conferencing, face-to-face, by email.

- How many clients do you want to have?

- What type of clients do you want to coach?

- How is your business going to affect your life"

- What does your typical work day look like?

- How many hours do you want to work in a day/week/month?

- How much money do you want to earn?

- What skills must you master?

- Are you going to do anything in addition to coaching? (teleseminars, workshops, etc)

- Are you going to create any products or write a book?

When working on defining your business dream make sure to answer as honestly as possibly but also think about if your dream is reflecting what you truly want and also if your dream inspires and motivates you. Sometimes we think we want something in a certain way but deep down we know it's rather wishful thinking and we really don't want it in the way we think we do. So keep that in mind when you define your dream. Only when you define your dreams in exactly the way you want can you achieve it.

Identifying Your Specialty Niche And Becoming An Expert

Once you defined your business dream you then should consider your specialty niche. The reason for why it is important to pick your niche is because it will be much easier to pinpoint your target market rather than being too broad. A specialty niche is a specific area you will be coaching in for example, I coach Holistic Life as well as Sales Acceleration, and because I chose two specific niches or specialties I can focus my marketing to specific people in those two areas. Advertising as "Life Coach" it is too vague and will make it more difficult to find clients because it is not targeted more specifically.

By deciding on a specialty niche you can develop a compelling message about the service you are offering which will assure that enough of the right people hear about your message. Your message would include things like who you coach, s your target market, and also your specialty or niche.

If you are not sure what area or specialty you want to focus on, think about your passions. If for example you are passionate about health and nutrition, weight loss or wellness coaching could be your niche. If you are familiar and passionate about business, sales or anything in that area, then becoming a business, executive, or sales coach might be the niche for you.

You might think that if you coach in multiple different areas you can get more clients, but unfortunately that is not the case because when it comes to effectively marketing your services. People hire professionals and when a person considers hiring a coach they don't think of it as "I need to find me a coach." No, they think something like "I would like to find a different job... I need to lose weight.... I need to reduce my stress.... I need to get back into shape." These are things people think about and when you tell them that you are a coach. They don't care about a coach; all they care about is their problems. When you position yourself as someone who can help them with their problem they then will start thinking "Maybe I should hire this person to help me with my problem".

Positioning yourself as an expert is a fundamental principal for marketing your services. If you needed a tooth pulled, you would not ask your plumber to pull your tooth right? We seek out professionals who can help us with our specific problem. This also applies to coaching; people hire a coach that is an expert in the area in which they need help.

When deciding on your niche, or area of expertise, you should focus on areas where you can provide value to clients. Chose a niche that people already have a need for and for which they are willing to pay. Here are a few examples of coaching niches:

Health and Wellness
- Losing weight
- Eating healthy
- Increasing fitness
- Reducing stress

Relationships
- Being a better parent
- Improving relationship with loved ones
- Having more social interactions

Love
- Finding Mr. or Mrs. Right
- Increasing romance and intimacy
- Developing a more fulfilling sex life

Business
- Increasing sales results
- Starting a new business
- Improving marketing strategies
- Increasing productivity

Career

- Transitioning into a new career
- Getting that promotion
- Learning skills to improve job performance

Money

- Getting out of debt
- Achieving financial freedom
- Increasing credit score

Time management

- Learning effective time management
- Overcoming procrastination
- Becoming more organized

To help you identify your specialty niche consider asking yourself questions like:

1. What is one thing that you are most passionate about? One thing that you could do or talk about all day without getting tired of it.

2. If you choose to write a book, what topic would you feel comfortable writing about?

3. What are some of your past interests, careers, things that you enjoyed doing or have a lot of knowledge about?

4. What obstacles have you successfully overcome, and how did you overcome them?

5. Which of your life experiences could others benefit from?

6. What talents or skills do you possess that you can leverage in your coaching?

7. Why did you become a coach?

Your Target Market and Ideal Client

Once you have identified and chosen your niche your next step is to identify your ideal client also called target market. It is very important to identify your ideal client because it will help you in marketing your services. First you should create your Ideal Client Profile as it relates to the type of person you want to coach, a person with whom you would feel most comfortable. You should define specific areas such as demographics, characteristics, buying history, and other important things relating to your niche.

For demographics define their gender, age, income, education, race, family status, profession, job status, job title, social affiliations, location, etc.

For personal characteristics define their interests, skills and abilities, beliefs, passions, traits, values, etc.

For their buying history define how they make buying decisions, how often they purchase online, what other related things they have invested or purchased, what seminars they attended, what books they read, etc.

Other things could be their annual revenue, their industry, number of employees, types of products or services sold, etc.

The main goal here is to clearly define your ideal client, that one type of person that would hire you as their coach because you are the one who has a solution to their specific problem.

Now it's time to create your professional statement of who you are and what you do. This is an essential part because it will help you in confidently communicating your coaching services. Most people don't really understand when you tell them that you are a coach or you are a ____ (your specialty) ____ coach. Because of the lack of understanding, it is important that you can clearly express what you do or otherwise you will be struggling with attracting clients and growing your business. Here is an example of a professional statement that clearly defines the "who" and the "what."

> *"I am a **Sales Acceleration** Coach. I work with **network marketers, coaches, and sales people** who **would like to increase their sales results and take their business/sales career to the next level**. My specialty is **working with those who are just starting out in business, struggling in business, or simply learning new ways to increase their sales results.**"*

If a person hears a statement like this they know right away who you are, what you do and most of all your area of expertise. However, if you simply state, "I am a Sales Acceleration Coach" they have no idea what exactly it is that you do. When talking to a prospective client, you want to sell the benefit or solution. You want to let the prospect know right away what it is you can help them with and if they are in sales and they hear this statement they automatically know that they would benefit from working with that coach.

I always ask my clients what they say when someone asks them what it is they do and they all tell me they say: I'm a Life Coach, I sell Avon Products, I'm a Sales Trainer, etc. It is true, this is what they do but when it comes to getting someone's interest you want to use the professional statement of telling them who you are and what you do….sell the solution not just what you do.

If you have more than one niche you would also have more than one target market and that's ok. What you can do is choose one as your primary target market and focus on investing enough time and energy on that one area to produce results. I'm not saying not to pay attention to your other target market but in order to get the best results you should not spread yourself too thin or otherwise you will have trouble getting a good return on your effort and marketing investment. In regards to your professional statement you could also focus on one primary niche; you can mention your secondary niche in your statement as well, or you can have two separate statements and pick the best one that best fits for the person with whom you are speaking.

Defining Your Coaching Process – How You Coach

Your coaching process simply describes your "how," How you coach your clients, and how you help them achieve the results they want. It basically explains how your coaching works. The "how you coach" is particularly important when explaining your coaching services to prospective clients or during the enrollment session because the prospect is going to want to know how you are going to help them achieve their goals. Your "How" needs to be clear and precise, yet simple enough for the prospect to completely understand your process. It should outline the steps you take during the coaching process.

Try not to give vague answers when someone inquires about your coaching process because that doesn't demonstrate confidence, and also does not help the person understand how you are helping others with your coaching.

Here is an example of a good "how" statement:

> *"I use a four-step coaching process with my clients. First I will help you identify how your life would look if you would have a successful, thriving, and fulfilling business. In order to attract something new into your life you must first be clear about what it is that you want. I have some powerful exercises that will help you gain real clarity and paint a very specific picture of your ideal business and life.*

Next, we identify at least three easy ways that you can experience more success and fulfillment with your life and business right now. This is often a lot simpler than you might think!

Building on your drive to succeed, I support you in creating your ideal business plan. The ideal business plan includes specific steps in two primary areas: eliminating the things that drain your energy and no longer serve you and putting new strategies and systems in place that will increase your sales results.

Finally, as your coach, I keep you focused, motivated and accountable as you implement your business plan. As you know, change isn't always easy. Setbacks can occur. Limiting beliefs may surface. Through our work together I'll help you overcome any challenges that may arise, enabling you to continue steadily forward as you build your business and become more successful. For success, you must act on them. I help you do that."

By defining your "how" and you not only help others understand how you coach but also build your credibility, which makes you successful. Once you have learned how to effortlessly, clearly and professionally explain your process, you will not only become more confident but you will also be seen as a credible professional.

Setting Your Pricing and Packaging

One reason why so many coaches are struggling financially is because they don't think they can charge that much. Many coaches base their fees on what they think is appropriate and feel most comfortable with but most of the time that amount is a lot lower than what they could be charging. Do you feel that asking for the money is already a dreaded part of selling your services but then asking for, let's say, $500 a month might seem too much? I assure you it is not. When you define your pricing packages there are many factors that influence your pricing, which includes the amount of training you have done, the number of sessions you will have with clients, the amount of support your clients get in between sessions, your target market and niche, and even your geographic location.

There are also other factors such as emotional and psychological factors which can influence your decision. Your self-belief and confidence in your abilities and the value of coaching that you are providing also play a big role when setting your pricing. Setting your fees too low can result in your becoming discouraged because you are not meeting your financial goal. If you set your price too high you might feel that you are not good enough to charge this much which will then cause your potential clients to not believe in your services.

When setting your pricing I want you to feel comfortable enough to charge what you deserve, according to the time and value you bring to the table. Consider how you can convince your potential clients to sign up for your coaching services and pay your fee regardless of how much you are charging, if you don't believe you are worth charging that amount. Many coaches who are just starting out charge very little which is okay in the beginning. I've met coaches who either don't charge at all for their services or very little because they don't think they are good enough to charge more. However, if you have done some coaching and training already, you already are more of an expert in coaching than the individuals you are coaching, which makes you the expert.

Most people judge the quality of the service by its price and you can just as easily lose a potential client by charging too little rather than charging too much. Consider this; if you see an ad in the papers or online where someone is offering professional life coaching services and they only charge fifty dollars per session, would you question that person's credibility? You would probably think that they are a newbie and just trying to find some clients. However, if you see an ad where someone offers their services at a rate of $150 an hour you probably think of that person as an expert because they are charging a much higher amount. It is all about perception. One very important thing to remember is, always position yourself as an expert; if you question your abilities than potential clients will do the same. Believe in yourself and your abilities because you have done the training, you have spent hours learning and practicing your skills and you are one step further than most of your clients because you have done the leg work of learning how to coach.

Another reason for setting your fees higher is because you will attract "serious" and "qualified" clients. There is a rule about service fees; the more the client has to pay, they more committed are they to make a change. If you only charge fifty dollars an hour you might get many clients but how effective will your coaching be? How motivated are these clients to really wanting to make a change? However, if they have to pay a good amount, you know they will put in the work and they will be happier with the results they are getting from coaching with you. If someone can't afford your fees than you have the option of either working out something with them (which I advise against) or you could offer group coaching or offer them your products.

The reason why you should not offer discounts to prospects who can't afford your coaching is because you could use that time more wisely and work on growing your business assets such as creating products, workshops, writing a book, publishing a newsletter, o public speaking, or any other activities that will help you grow your business.

There are typically two ways coaches charge for their services — monthly or hourly per session. Charging monthly might be the easiest way and if you are using a merchant service to charge them it will also be less expensive because with a merchant service you do not have to pay per transaction. You can also set to charge your clients automatically which will be easier on you because you don't have to remember to charge their cards or send them an invoice. When choosing your pricing packages, set two to three different pricing models. The different pricing models could be a low-priced package, a medium-priced package and a high-priced package.

The high-priced could be your premium package where they get the maximum level of service. The medium package is for clients who want to be coached but simply can't afford your premium package. The low-priced package is designed for clients who want to try coaching to see how they like it and are not willing to make such a big investment until they know for sure that coaching is for them.

Below is an example of such a pricing model. As you can see, the highest priced model also offers the most number of sessions as well as the best support out of all packages, whereas the lowest package doesn't have too much to offer other than the trial sessions.

Premium Package - $495 per month

- Weekly calls for forty-five minutes
- Unlimited pone, text and email access
- Post session email report with recording of session

Medium Package - $300 per month

- Three forty-five minute calls a month
- Unlimited pone, text and email access
- Recorded calls

Starter Package - $225 per month

- Two forty-five minute calls a month
- Limited phone, text and email access (one contact per week)

When explaining your fees, start out with the premium package then the middle, and finally the lowest package. The reason for starting with the premium package is because that's the one you want to sell, and the middle and lowest packages are really just for those who are interested in coaching but simply can't afford your other packages. Also, it is important to include what they get with each package. Not only mention the price but also how many calls they get each month, and what other services they get with each package. But remember, when going over your fees, don't rush through it, speak slowly and clearly so your prospect understands what each package entails. If you speak too fast and rush through your pricing packages, the prospect will less likely be able to make a sound buying decision..

Business Start Up Requirements

In order to operate a coaching business, or any business, there are other requirements needed to be put in place for a smooth operation. There is the front end of your coaching business which is the coaching itself but there is also the backend of your coaching business which involves running and maintaining your business. The following items are things you need to operate your business. You don't need to implement all at once but they are necessary.

- A written description of what you want your business to look like
- A name for your business
- A professional-looking business card

- An information sheet or brochure to give to potential clients (hard copy and digital)
- A welcome package
- A written coaching agreement document
- A computer with Internet access
- A professional email address (no Gmail, yahoo, Hotmail, etc)
- A separate phone line or cell phone for business
- A quality headset
- A professional-sounding voice mail answering message
- A separate checking account solely used for business, and check book for this account
- A separate credit card solely used for business
- A merchant account to accept payments
- A CPA or bookkeeper
- An accounting software application
- Registered business structure (sole proprietor, LLC, S-Corp.)
- Registered business name within town/city of operation
- Any business license if necessary
- Insurance coverage (liability, errors and omissions, disability, health)
- Dedicated office space/area either in your home or outside of your home
- Printer, Fax, Scanner
- Office Supplies

Your Business Plan

If you are wondering why you should have a business plan for your coaching business, it's simple. Even the smallest business should have and can benefit from having a business plan in place. A business plan is your business roadmap; it includes your vision for your business, as well as a thorough market research and detailed information about your marketing strategies, your target audience, and any staff you might consider having in the future, as well as obstacles and goals. It will also include an executive summary which is a brief summary of the entire plan you have for your business.

Even though putting together your business plan takes some work to complete but if you remember the part about defining your dream and goal setting, you must write down what you want and be as specific as you can. This is exactly what a business plan is. A business plan will also help you identify what works and what doesn't because it is an open document. You never really complete it because you always add to it and remove things that simply don't fulfill their purpose; you change things around and modify it every time something changes about your vision for your business.

If you are not familiar with how to write a business plan, the Small Business Association (SBA) offers a tool that will help you create your business plan. Visit **http://bit.ly/BusinessPlanTool**

Ways To Coach

One great aspect about coaching is that you have the ability to coach in different ways from coaching someone face to face and one on one, to group coaching, offering workshops, offering mastermind groups, and also offering training and certification programs.

Coaching One-on-One

When coaching someone one-on-one, you can do it by phone, email, video conferencing or face-to-face. This form of coaching is very rewarding because you can connect with your client on a deeper level. However, if you only rely on one-on-one coaching, you might not be able to earn as much as you would like because you are limited to the amount of clients you can serve each day.

Each session usually runs about forty-five minutes to an hour but you also need time to prepare before the call and you might need a break after the call to ground yourself before getting ready for the next call. Technically you would need to a two-hour block for each client which will allow you to coach four to six clients a day if you are coaching full-time. However, you also need to find the time to market your business, be active on social media to build up your reputation, make cold calls to get new clients, and perform bookkeeping and other administrative duties.

Group Coaching

Group coaching, on the other hand is a great addition to one-on-one coaching which allows for earning a higher amount in less time because you can coach a number of people all at the same time. This type of coaching won't allow you to connect with your clients as deeply as with your one-on-one clients but you still will be able to make a big difference in their lives and you can also offer one-on-one coaching for those who would like additional, more targeted coaching. Group coaching can be done face-to-face, by phone, or via video conferencing.

Workshops

Workshops are similar to group coaching; however, during a workshop you would be teaching your clients on a topic in your specialty niche. For example, *"Twelves steps to a healthier you"*, or *"Learn how to increase your sales results in this three-hour workshop"*. Workshops are all about content; they provide the participants with steps on what they need to do to make a particular change, i.e. increasing their sales results, getting healthy, etc. Giving workshops is also a great way for generating leads because after the workshop you can contact each of the participants and offer your coaching services. It also lets people know that you are an expert in that particular field or area in which you are coaching. If you don't feel comfortable in front of the room you could even offer these workshops online as webinars or also tele-workshops. You have the option to charge for these workshops or offer them for free if you are mainly interested in getting leads.

Mastermind Group Coaching

The concept of the Mastermind Group was initially introduced by Napoleon Hill who wrote the book *Think and Grow Rich*. He describes Mastermind Groups as something where multiple great minds get together to share their knowledge about their area of expertise and their experience. If for example you are a Health and Wellness Coach and you are holding Mastermind Groups, you would invite one or two other experts in the same niche to share some valuable information with the group.

But be advised, no selling of other services should take place during these sessions. Mastermind Groups is all about providing valuable content to all participants. Inviting experts to share their knowledge is also great exposure and the participants can connect with them if they choose. These Mastermind Groups can also be helpful as tele-conferences which will allow individuals nationwide and even worldwide to attend. You can charge a fee for this group or you can have it as part of your regular coaching or product fee.

Training Coaching

If you enjoy coaching large groups you could consider offering training coaching where you offer coaching to larger organizations to train their staff. Most of the coaching will be done either on stage or in a classroom setting. You could also offer additional group coaching to those who are interested in additional support for implementing what you taught, or you could offer individual coaching to those who are interested in high-level support. Consider high level coaches such as Tony Robbins, Brian Tracy, or Eric Lofholm. They all have their own team of coaches who work with their attendees.

Membership Coaching

Membership Coaching is probably the most lucrative way of offering your services because your clients would be paying a monthly fee to gain access to all of your services and products. This model allows you to deliver value in other ways besides coaching. You can have a members only forum, you can invite experts to share their knowledge (i.e. Mastermind Group), if you have created any products members would have access to those as well, and you can offer other helpful resources inside the member area.

This model is much more flexible than the other models because members can access the material 24/7 without your having to be present. Individuals can sign up without your having to do any kind of selling but you can enjoy consistent residual income every month.

***

When determining your coaching model, think about the level of energy that is required for each activity to put together your coaching model which best fits your need and desired income. Remember, you do not have to choose only one model, you can use multiple or even all of the models.

MARKETING YOUR COACHING PRACTICE

Develop your marketing strategy

If you are already an experienced coach who has made a name for themselves congratulations. However, if you are just starting out, your situation is different because no one knows about you and what you have to offer. As a new coach it will take some time to make a name for yourself and it will also take some time to find a good number of clients because you have zero visibility; no one knows you even exist. Unfortunately many coaches stay invisible even years after they launch their coaching business because they are either lacking the confidence of their abilities, they may not think they are ready to be seen as an expert, or they might be afraid that they would fail. Some might also have trouble positioning themselves as an expert or have trouble identifying and effectively marketing to their target market.

If you want to have a successful and profitable coaching business you must be bold enough to declare you are an expert in your niche. You must be pro-active and reach out to your target market; don't wait for them to come to you, reach out, generate leads, make contact, and conduct complimentary coaching sessions. Don't give up if things get tough. The key is to be persistent and continue doing what you are doing.

Different ways to market your coaching business

There are many different ways to market your coaching business; unfortunately you can't do them all but if you have the funds available you can definitely try different ones and pick the ones that produce the best results. However, if you are just starting out, use low-cost and practical ways to get your clients. Marketing strategies can quickly run you in the negative if you don't have enough money coming in to cover all the expenses. When you are first starting out you might also have to do some of the leg work like passing out flyers. There are a few marketing strategies that can help you make a name for yourself.

Marketing Materials

Business Cards

A business card serves as a contact reference for your business. Passing out your business card to potential clients is very helpful and they are a lot more convenient and professional.

Brochures

A well-designed brochure is an excellent addition to information packages to present your services. Inserting a brochure in newspapers, letters, or even placing them in your office or at different locations will inform people about your coaching services, or products you have to offer.

Flyers

A flyer is a great way of announcing your event, including workshops, complimentary coaching sessions, tele-seminars, or group coaching.

Grassroot Marketing

Grassroot marketing strategies are relatively inexpensive but can be very effective because they consist of reaching out to friends and family, taking advertising to the potential customers through passing out flyers, placing business cards or brochures, in different businesses. This strategy is especially beneficial for coaches who are just starting out or who have been having trouble getting their name out. Instead of launching a message in hope of reaching many people, you would target your efforts to a smaller group hoping they will spread the word to their network of people.

Networking

Networking is also a very effective but time-consuming marketing strategy because it consists of attending different networking events to connect with people and to exchange business cards or contact information. One problem with new coaches is that they don't have the time to attend networking events because most of those events are held during the day while people are usually at work. However, if you do have the time to go to events, this is a great way of connecting with others. You may even be able to meet people to build joint ventures with or reciprocal referral relationships.

Referrals

Referrals are a great way of getting new leads from your already satisfied clients. You will learn about Referral Strategy in Part III of this book, a strategy that is guaranteed to get you referrals. The benefit of referrals is that people will be calling you or you will get quality leads from your clients which minimizes your efforts of finding new leads. Choosing to include referrals into your marketing strategy is an excellent choice.

Speaking Engagements

Speaking engagements is possibly the most powerful and most effective lead generation strategy because you position yourself as an expert and people can hear you speak and it gives you great exposure. Even though you might not feel very comfortable about speaking in front of a large group of people, you might want to consider implementing speaking engagements at a later time. If you do incorporate speaking engagements into your marketing strategy join a Toastmaster group in your area where you will learn how to effectively give speeches.

The main reason why speaking is so powerful is because it allows you to show off what you know, and people will view you as an expert. You have an opportunity to provide value to your audience and give them an experience of how powerful, knowledge, and caring you are and that you are truly interested in help solving their problems.

Speaking engagements can have different forms, from giving a presentation, workshops, seminars, webinars, teleclasses, meetup groups, informal talks to being a guest speaker at someone else's event or conference.

The benefits of speaking engagements not only include positioning yourself as an expert providing increased exposure because you are not only presenting your services to one person but to a large number of individuals. When you first start out offering speaking engagements you may not have a large audience but once you have given a few, the word about you will go around and if you have provided enough value in previous engagements more people will starting to sign up for your events.

Of course when you speak, your audience will be able to experience who you are and what you are about. Speaking engagements are also a great way of building you list of prospective clients because every time you speak, you invite your audience to join your mailing list and you can contact them after the event to offer a complimentary coaching session as a thank you.

Strategic Alliances

A strategic alliance is a relationship formed between you and one or more entities that agree to share resources to achieve mutual benefits, meaning both parties get something out of the relationship. Forming strategic alliances is possibly the one strategy that could fill your entire coaching practice. By forming relationships with others you have the potential to secure dozens of clients. Even though forming strategic alliances might not be an easy task to complete if you know someone that has your target market in their network, you could connect with them and form an alliance. For example offer free coaching or seminars to their team or something that would be of value to the person with whom you are planning to form a strategic alliance.

Forming such alliances requires effort from your part, discipline to follow through and most of all a significant level of professionalism and structure. The relationship between you and the strategic alliance partner should be a win-win type of relationship where all parties, this includes both you and the partner as well as the potential coaching clients, get something out of it.

The most important part about strategic alliances is that it all must be handled very professionally. You should have some sort of documentation that defines everything that was agreed on between you and the strategic alliance partner. Remember, you are forming a professional partnership or professional relationship.

In order for the strategic alliance to be most effective you should have some sort of system in place where the partner can send or refer their people. The referring process is meant to become a part of their business process. To secure such a strategic alliance, \ define what type of partner you are looking for, one that best fits your needs and most of all that has your target market in their network. Clearly define what you can bring to the table as far as your strength, your services, etc. Strategic alliances have both advantages and disadvantages. Some of the advantages are that you can relatively quickly fill your coaching practice if you form a strategic alliance with the right type of individuals or businesses. You can also leverage their resources and knowledge and most of all have easier access to new opportunities with less effort and obstacles.

The disadvantages of strategic alliances are that implementing and managing such alliances may be difficult and time consuming because each partner has their own way of operating. Both you and the strategic alliance partner could not be satisfied with what each of you gets out of the relationship.

It is also possible that each of you could become more dependent on the other partner which can make it difficult to operate as separate entities if the relationship would end. Strategic alliances are built on trust and it takes time and effort to establish and nurture such relationships, especially at the beginning.

List Building

The best way to explain the importance of building your list is "The Money Is in the List!" What that means is, if you are serious about making money with your coaching business you have to build your list. Without a list of people to market to, you will not be making any money. In order to start building your list you would need something that's called an opt-in list or opt-in form which you can place on your website, your blog, social media sites or as a link in your email signature.

Don't disregard this, because if you do, you will have a very hard time getting clients unless you want to spend money on buying leads or looking through the phone book. By having an opt-in option you will be able to capture qualified leads, individuals who already showed interest in you and your services.

In order to have a properly working list there are different components required to collect leads effectively. These components are an opt-in form, an auto responder service, something of value that you give away for free and a database to handle and manage your list. Let's look at each component a little bit closer.

Opt-in Form

The opt-in form is required to capture the user's information. If you are unfamiliar with what opt-in means, it is simply a tool that allows potential clients to self-select to subscribe to your mailing list. When someone enters their information into an opt-in or sign up form, they give you the permission to send them marketing materials. E-mail newsletters for example are an opt-in or subscription form, where you enter your information to get information.

Now that we have determined what opt-in means, let's take a look at how you can set up such an opt-in form. An inexpensive service is GetResponse; this online service provides everything needed to collect and manage leads. It also has other features such as auto responder, landing page creator, and email marketing. There are other form builders available online but GetResponse is most valuable in regards to ease of use and monthly service fee.

Auto responder

An auto responder is an automatic email service which allows you to set up pre-written messages which will be sent to recipients on a scheduled basis. For instance, if someone opts-in or signs up for your monthly newsletter, you could use the auto responder to send a welcome email as soon as they sign up.

With an auto responder you can also send follow-up emails, birthday messages, as well as customized offers to those on your list. An auto responder allows you to automate part of your communication with potential clients and build rapport when they get a thank you or welcome email.

There are two types of auto responder services, one is the single opt-in and the other one is double opt-in. However, the best one to get is the double-opt in because it requires the user to opt in twice. What that means is, once a user enters their information into the opt-in form (first opt-in) they will receive an email to the email address they signed up with, to confirm the subscription (second opt-in).

If they user does not confirm the subscription their name will not show up on your list of subscribers. The reason why the double opt-in service is better is because it weeds out the good from the bad and you will not be getting any wrong contact information.

The single opt-in service only requires the user to enter their information into the opt-in form and their name and email will show up on your list of subscribers. However, you would not be certain if the information they have entered is correct because no email was sent to the email address they have provided to confirm that it is a valid email address. One way to use the single opt-in option would be for contact forms which don't require a subscription.

Valuable content

The best way to collect leads through opt-in is by giving away something for free. This could be a free report, a free video with valuable information, a free consultation, or anything else that you can think of which will provide value to the individual without selling your services. Let's say you are in health and wellness and you specialize in weight loss. You could write a report or article on healthy nutrition or exercising tips.

The point here is to provide nothing but valuable content to the individual. The offer has to be valuable enough for them to give you their information. Remember this, their thought pattern is: "What's in it for me?" Your free item has to satisfy their desire or need for your information. By giving away something for free you also allow the individuals to get a taste of what you have to offer, and shed light on your level of expertise. It will also position you as "the expert".

List management

Managing your list of subscribers is very important to build and maintain a relationship with your list. When someone signs up for your newsletter they expect to receive valuable information from you consistently. You have the option to manage your list yourself or you could also hire someone, a virtual assistant for example, to maintain and manage your list..

Now that you have learned about the different components required to build your list, let's talk about how you can start building your list. One very effective way of building your lists is through teleseminars or webinars. Every time someone signs up or registers to attend your seminar their names would go into your database of leads. You can also invite the attendees during the seminar or webinar to sign up for your newsletter. Another way of building your list is through increasing traffic to your website either through paid ads, passing out flyers with the offer for the free item, and also through social media posts.

Another option would be to have a call to action in your email signature which directs people to visit your site for your free item or to sign up for your "life changing" newsletter. For example: "To receive your free report on *How to manage stress at your workplace*" go to **http://www.yourdomainname.com.**"

You could pass around a signup sheet and anyone who would like to either sign up for your newsletter or to receive additional information would write down their information.

One great way of building your list is by using different social media sites such as Facebook, LinkedIn, and Twitter. The only downfall with social media marketing is you have to be very active and consistently provide a lot of valuable content to make a name for yourself. If you only post every once in a while, users would not consider you as an expert and less likely respond to your offers.

This type of list building is considered a "high-touch" marketing strategy because it requires a high level of interaction on your part. However, it can be very effective and once you have built your reputation of being "an expert" and you make a name for yourself, it will not take as much effort as it does when first starting out.

Website

If at one point you thought having a website was not that important to grow your business and that you don't need to have a website, let me tell you that is wrong. In today's time or technology, not having a website or a web presence can be your downfall. It is extremely important to have at least a basic website so people can see who you are and what you do. A website gives you instant credibility. It allows people from all over the world to reach out to you, and if you have created products that you are selling, think about it, you could be making money 24/7 without having to do anything to generate income.

Let me ask you this, think back, the last time someone gave you a business card, or you saw a poster or flyer with someone offering a specific service and you wanted to learn more, did you just pick up the phone and call them or did you first look up their website to get more information to make the decision to reach out to them?

As a coach you are selling a service that can't be touched or looked at which makes it even more important to have a website because it represents you and what you are offering; it makes you and your services seem real. No one wants to buy something they know nothing about. Right? This is why it is important that the content you create for your website is professionally written. The content is the foundation to prepare the rest of your marketing materials. It forces you to really think about what exactly it is that you are offering, your pricing models, the way you coach, and a website is like a digital brochure or catalog that represents your services.

Building a website can be an overwhelming task because you have to consider creating your website yourself or paying someone to create it for you. If you are not very technical and you have no idea how to create a website it would be best if you hire someone to create your site for you. However, paying someone to do your site can become pricey; the best thing to do is shop around, get quotes from different web designing companies and pick the one that best fits your needs and your wallet.

Launching your website can be a big project but one of keys to having a successful website is to determine how "big" you want your website to be. How "big" is beneficial for you? If you are launching your very first website, start out with a basic website. In the future you can always add to your site, according to what your business needs are.

Step 1 - Basic Website

The basic website is basically an electronic brochure of your coaching practice and should include the following:

- Home Page – the home page is an introduction of what you do; think of it as the back matter of a book that gives you a short introduction about the book.

- Coaching Services Page – on this page you would elaborate about your coaching services, your niche, how you conduct sessions, etc.

- About Page – this page is where you would put your biography, telling the client more about you and your experience as a coach and what you bring to the table.

- Contact Page – this page is very important because it allows potential clients to reach out to you. On this page you could either write your contact information such as phone number or email address, or you could also put a contact form where the individual enters a message directly on your page and once they click submit it goes directly into your email inbox. You can do either or, or you can have both ways to contact you on your page.

- Newsletter Sign-up Form – this could be a separate page or just a form placed on the home page or somewhere else on your website; just make sure it is visible and easy to find.

- Thank you Page – this is the page the user is redirected to once they sign up for your newsletter.

- Message Sent – This page is where the user is redirected once they submit the contact request form.

- Success Stories – if you already have success stories I would recommend adding those to your site because nothing sells better than success. If your visitors see success stories they will already see you in a different light.

- FAQs Page – to answer any questions a possible client may have about coaching and your services.

- Fees/Pricing – you should have a list of your fees listed on your website so visitors can see if they can even afford your services. This weeds out the good from the bad.

- Blog – not necessarily needed but most definitely a valuable option to include on your website. A blog allows you to share valuable content with your clients and visitors which display your level of knowledge and expertise. However, if you do decide to have a blog, add content consistently. for example once a month.

These are the most important parts to a basic website and if you are just starting out you really don't need anything more than a basic site.

Step 2 – More Advanced Website

Once you have created products, recorded teleseminars, webinars, etc you then can upgrade your site with those items. The more advanced website or what I call a step 2 website, includes the following, and is an upgrade to the Step 1 website:

- More valuable content – this could be resources, additional reports, audio and video clips, articles, etc.

- Calendar of Events – this will allow you to post all upcoming events on your website for everyone who visits your site to see. For example you have an upcoming webinar scheduled; someone visiting your site will find out about the event and give them the option to sign up.

- Discussion Boards – this allows clients and potential clients to interact with each other and also ask questions, get help and support, etc.

- More interaction – adding an assessment for example, or a questionnaire

- Blog – not necessarily needed for the Step 1 website but should most definitely be part of the Step 2 website.

As you can see the Step 2 website has more to offer than the Step 1 website; however, when choosing which type of website you want, first define your exact needs and what you want your website to do and how advanced is beneficial for you at that moment.

Step 3 - Advanced Website

The Step 1 and Step 2 websites are still relatively basic sites whereas the Step 3 website has a lot more to offer and would be beneficial for those coaches who want to sell their products online. The Step 3 website would include the following additions:

- Selling physical products – this could be physical products such as books, booklets, CDs, DVDs, or any other physical products you have created.

- Selling digital products – this could be any e-books, e-courses, digital workshops, etc.

- Membership sites – if you have multiple products you could offer membership packages where members have access to all of your products at one time or also monthly fee.

- Affiliate program – if you are selling products you could offer an affiliate program so others can sell your products, services, memberships and earn a certain percentage when they make a sale.

- Online appointment setting application – this will allow potential clients to schedule an appointment through your website without even having to talk to you; once they sign up you will be notified and it will show up on your calendar.

- Online payment options – offering credit card payments for your products and also your coaching services. Individuals could also purchase your coaching services through your website.

Now that you know about the different types of websites, it is time to decide on which website type would best fit your needs and your wallet. This can be very frustrating because many coaches, especially those who are just starting out, simply don't have the budget or a limited budget for a website. Some even decide to go ahead and do it themselves which is fine.

However, one word of advice; if you have no idea about creating a website, I strongly suggest to save up the money and pay someone to create the site for you. It can take you a very long time trying to figure out everything you need to do and everything you need to watch out for when creating a website. Most novices do not know about the law in regards to using content and images they find online, it can happen that they end up violating copyright law because they use content or images they found online.

Let's talk about additional things you need to launch your website. Once you have decided what type of website you want, and if you are going to build your website yourself or if you are going to hire someone to build the website for you, you would have to decide on a domain name for you site; many use either their business name or their own name but this is completely up to you. However, it should be something professional and something that reflect or represents your coaching services.

Once you decided on a name you would purchase your domain name. You could go to GoDaddy.com or HostGator.com to purchase your domain name. It is possible that your particular domain name is not available with the type of extension you would like such as .com, .net, .info, etc. In that case you would have to come up with a different name or a different variation. But be advised, if you chose a variation of the name you initially had decided on but there is a similar domain name already out there, there is always a chance that people accidentally go to that other website instead of yours. Just keep that in mind when deciding on a domain name.

Once you have a domain name, you also need to purchase webhosting. There are many different webhosting companies available but one most are familiar with is HostGators webhosting services but GoDaddy also has great webhosting packages.

If you are still debating about creating your own website ask yourself the following questions:

- Do you enjoy computers and technology?

- Do you enjoy learning new things about technology?

- Do you want to spend hours learning about building your website and then creating your website?

- Do you think it is wise spending all this time learning about how to create websites and actually creating your site instead of building your business and getting clients?

- Do you want to be in control of your website?

- Do you want to be responsible for updating and maintaining your website?

- Are you familiar with Photoshop to create graphics needed for your site?

If you answered yes to these questions you would enjoy creating your site yourself. However, if you said no to any or all of these questions hire someone to do it for you or you end up getting frustrated and you waste a lot of time.

If you do decide to hire someone, create your plan for your website. Determine your budget and create a list of things you want on your website as well as what content you would like to have added. Think about the main theme for your site, what colors you would like, how many opt-in forms, what you want to offer, how soon you would want the site to go live, any images you would like to use. Get all these things together prior to meeting or speaking with the Web Designer.

Creating your own website is not an easy task so visit my Desktop Publishing site **www.uronestop.com** where I offer affordable web and graphic design services. I have a team of highly professional web and graphic designers who provide outstanding services at a very reasonable price.

Landing Page/Squeeze Page

A landing page is similar to a website with one major difference. It is only a single page, and it does not have a menu bar where visitors can browse through the different pages like with a regular website. The sole purpose of a Landing Page or Squeeze Page is to generate leads. A Landing Page usually offers something for free with the sole purpose of the visitor entering their contact information, usually their name and email, in order to get a free report, access to an exclusive video, or anything else of value. It is similar to an opt-in form on your website but the landing page would have its own domain name and is a standalone lead generation page. You would not add any personal information, a contact page, information about your services or anything in that matter. The only information that goes on a Landing Page is the information for the free item the user gets when entering their information.

I am sure you have come across a sales page which is one very long page with a lot of information about one particular product and at the bottom there is the call to action, which is usually asking you to buy the product. However, for a Landing Page, the call to action would not be asking the visitor to pay; instead the call to action is entering their information to get the free item.

Once someone enters their information their name and email would be added to your database and you then can start marketing to them. Having a landing page is a great way to generate leads because you can have marketing material specifically driving traffic to that one site, you could hand out flyers with the link to your landing page, or you could also add the link to your email signature. There are many different ways to advertise your landing page.

A landing page is not a necessity to building your business, but it would definitely help in building your list.

Blogging

A blog is simply a standalone website or part of your website where you can share content in the form of articles, also known as blog posts. These articles are intended to be informative, entertaining, or have a specific purpose. You could blog about specific topics in your niche; for example if you are a finance coach you could be sharing valuable tips about ways to save money, or how to become debt free.

The main purpose of blogging is to provide valuable information to those who are visiting your site and also your clients. It allows you to position yourself as an expert where you can show your visitors how much you know and that you possibly have the answer or solution to their problem. You could even redirect your clients or any prospective clients to your website to get answers on certain questions they might have on specific topics.

Having a blog on your website will also help you drive traffic to your site because blogs are automatically optimized for search engines. SEO or search engine optimization is a critical part to increasing traffic to your site. Google robots crawl and index your website every so often on the search for new and fresh content; they also look for frequent updates, but if they don't find any new content, your search engine page ranking decreases. However, if you consistently and regularly add new content to your blog, it will increase your ranking.

In your blog posts you can incorporate keywords which the search engine picks up on which gives you a higher ranking in the search engines. If you consistently update your blog, this will increase your visibility online and also improve your SEO and search engine page ranking. To increase your search engine ranking include relevant keywords within the content of your blog posts such as within the title, within the description, the headings, category names, trackback links, and even comment invitations.

Blog posts also provide great content which can be shared across social networks, which also keeps visitors interested in returning to your site. However, if you decide to start a blog or add a blog to your site, in order to take full advantage of the benefits, make it a habit to consistently post new and valuable content to your blog. When you define your marketing strategy, determine how often you are going to post to your blog, once a month, once every two months, every other week, or weekly.

Once you decide how often you want to blog, stick with it; don't start blogging every week and then stop for a month or two. In order for your blog to be most beneficial, you must be consistent. With that said if you have trouble coming up with all the content to write on your blog, you can choose to only post once a month or once every two months. The key point here is, if you decide to post once a month, make it a habit to post every month around the same time. If you have trouble remembering, put a reminder in your phone or on your calendar.

Blogging has become the new and better marketing strategy compared to the traditional or old-fashioned way of marketing. It is more interactive than newsletters or emails, because if your blog posts are interesting and informative, your readers are more likely to engage, post replies and even share your blog post on their social networking sites.

To set up your blog you can choose to have a standalone blog or as part of your website; if you decide to have a standalone blog you would also need a separate domain name. One of the best and most used blogging platforms is Wordpress. Wordpress is relatively easy to set up. Many different plug-ins are available which you can upload and use with your blog or website.

If you don't feel up to the task of consistently and regularly spending time on your blog, hire a Virtual Assistant who can post on your blog for you. You could even pay someone to write the posts for you if you are not too fond of writing. Consider including blogging into your marketing strategy to position yourself as an expert and also to increase your search engine page ranking. Just because you have a website does not mean you automatically get tons of visitors. You have to drive traffic to your site and the best way to do so is to implement a blog and be actively posting new content.

Newsletters

A newsletter is similar to a newspaper, only digital and a lot smaller and less content. The core benefit of offering your clients or prospective clients a newsletter is to keep your brand, in your case your coaching services, in front of individuals who are interested as well as your clients. A newsletter assists in getting and maintaining the attention from your subscribers. You could for example send out a monthly newsletter with "how-to" tips relating to your specialty niche.

A newsletter also allows you to send out periodic updates, promotions, news, and even event notifications. While you may not get any immediate business from sending out newsletters, your subscribers at least won't forget about you and eventually they might reach out to you because they have come to that point in their lives where they would benefit from your coaching services. Businesses used to stay in touch with their clients through print mailings, but electronic versions are more effective and greatly reduce the cost involved with printing and postage.

Ezine Articles

Ezines is another great marketing strategy that can help you in increasing traffic to your site. As mentioned before, just because you have a website does not mean you automatically get visitors. Marketing and driving traffic to your site is all about exposure and link building, having an online presence in different locations with links to your site. Most of the time when someone does visit your site, the retention rate is very low, as is the return rate. What that means is, those who find their way to your website may skim through and leave your site to never return again. Just having a website simply doesn't cut it anymore in today's day and age.

To turn things around and to increase the amount of visitors coming and most of all staying and returning to your site, an Ezine might be the answer. If you are not sure what an Ezine is, it is similar to a newsletter but there are online services out there such as Ezinearticles.com that allow you to post your articles online on their server for everyone to see. Online Ezine publishing services are very beneficial because your articles are managed and designed to give you maximum exposure.

Well-established services such as Ezinearticles.com already have a large audience which will help your visibility. Submitting Ezine articles will also give you a boost in credibility and position yourself as an expert. You can include a short introduction at the bottom of your Ezines as well as promotional offers and call to actions to redirect visitors to your website.

The difference between newsletters and Ezine articles is that you have to have your own list of people to whom you can send the newsletter. Ezine articles on the other hand are submitted online for everyone to see. You don't have to have a list in order to share your knowledge with others.

However, Ezines will assist you in building your lists because if someone sees your article and is interested in learning more, they would go visit your site. If you have a call to action opt-in form on your home page, the individual is more likely to input their information because you have already demonstrated your knowledge in your article. Also, if your articles are posted on sites such as Ezinearticles.com, you already have an instant credibility because your article was approved as something valuable.

Here are some suggestions for getting started with your Ezines. First design your Ezine template; you can also purchase a template package on Ezinearticles.com which will help you with everything you need to post a valuable Ezine article.

Once you have decided on your template, use this template for all the articles you submit, so readers recognize your brand. Next decide on an Ezine service. If you are sending the Ezine to your list, do not attempt to send out mass emails with your regular email service, or there is a possibility that you would get banned for spamming. Instead use services such as MailChimp, AWeber, or online Ezine services such as Ezine Articles, just to name a few. Feel free to do your own research for the service that best fits your needs.

If you choose a mailing service where you mail out your Ezine, you always have to worry about your mail landing in your subscribers SPAM folders rather than their inbox. Instead of sending out your Ezine, you could post them online and simply inform your list of the article you posted recently and send them the link. You could also share the link on your social networking sites for greater exposure.

When deciding on your Ezine, choose a topic that represents the number one reason for your target market frustration or problem. For example, if you are a health and wellness coach, your target clients deal with different issues such as nutrition, stress, obesity, and work and life imbalance.

In order to get your target markets attention you could chose topics such as: "Ten steps to a less stressful life", or "Five easy steps to achieve work/life balance". The point here is to pick topics that will catch the reader's interest. Remember the goal of an Ezine is to build relationships and to drive traffic to your site. It is not about getting immediate sales; you first have to build your reputation and let people see that you are an expert.

Teleclasses/Webinars

Teleclasses or Webinars are a great way to get new coaching clients as well as to sell your products. Many coaches take advantage of the benefits that come with offering teleclasses or seminars because they are able to reach a larger number or individuals because people all over the world can attend such seminars or classes. The difference between teleclass and webinars is that a teleclass is conducted over the phone, with no visual aids. All participants simply call into a special conference bridge where the host has the control to either mute the entire call so only he or she can be heard, or the line can be left open to allow for discussions and participations of the attendees.

Webinars on the other hand are conducted online through online presentation services where visual aids are used. Webinars might be more interactive and interesting because the attendees have something to look at whereas at a teleseminar the attendees are on the phone with no visual aids which can lead to attendees being less interested.

Either way of presenting your coaching services or your products are beneficial because you do get qualified leads. Every person who signs up for your workshop is a qualified lead and you can offer them your coaching services or you could offer everyone who attended or who signed up for the workshop a complimentary coaching session. As you already know, speaking engagements are one of the best ways to present yourself as the expert and to get new clients.

However, speaking in front of a large group of people is not for everyone, and if you are one of those individuals who does not enjoy public speaking, you are not the only one. This is why conducting workshops through teleseminars or webinars is beneficial because you get to speak to a large group of people but behind the scene. When you conduct these workshops, your attendees will not see you, but hear you. This might bring you some peace of mind because the good thing about doing teleseminars or webinars is that you can read your script word for word without having to worry about forgetting what you were going to say next because you are too nervous to keep a clear head.

On a side note, if you do read your presentation, make sure you practice your presentation multiple times prior to giving your presentation to make sure you don't sound like you are reading your script.

You can choose to conduct your workshops to be interactive where you involve your attendees or you can choose to teach your workshop similar to a lecture where you are the only one who speaks and your attendees just listen. You can also send your attendees materials and activities to use throughout the workshop, prior to the workshop.

To promote your teleclass or webinar you would start promoting about a month prior to the scheduled date for the workshop. Promoting too close to the scheduled date, you might not be able to fill your workshop. This is why it is important to start about a month prior to the scheduled date; this will allow you to advertise in different ways to reach enough individuals.

SETTING YOUR SERVICE GOALS

The most important part of becoming successful in your business is to set a goal for yourself. Only if you have a set goal will you be able to achieve great things. We had talked about defining your overall business goals but in this section we will talk about setting your service goals. Your service goal defines how many complimentary coaching sessions do you want to conduct in a specific time frame and how many clients to you want to have. By setting your service goals it will help you get into action and it will help you do what you know you need to be doing to reach your goal.

Every successful sales person has a set goal of how many calls they make each day, how many appointments they run each day and week, how many appointments they have to run to close on the number of new clients they want to gain, how much money they want to earn in a month and year, and what all they have to do to accomplish what they set out to do.

Let me ask you this, how many clients would like to have within the next ninety days? Write down how many clients do you want to have ninety days from today. Next, think about how many Complimentary Coaching Sessions would you have to conduct to secure the number of new clients you just wrote down? Let's say you would like ten new clients within ninety days and your closing ration is one out of five.

The way to calculate how many Complimentary Coaching Sessions you have to conduct to get your ten clients within the next ninety days is the following:

_____ new clients * _____ Complimentary Coaching Session to gain one new clients = _____ sessions in ninety days

Ten new coaching clients multiplied by five Complimentary Coaching Sessions to get one new client, equals fifty Complimentary Coaching Sessions. So over the next ninety days to reach your goal of gaining ten new coaching clients, you would have to conduct fifty Complimentary Coaching Sessions. Once you determine how many sessions you need to conduct over the next ninety days, you would next determine how many sessions you need to conduct each month and each week.

As you determined how many sessions you need over the ninety days, each month, and each week, write down your service goals in a sentence.

I _____ *will conduct*
_____ *Complimentary Coaching Sessions within the next*
ninety days to gain _____ *new coaching clients. Over the next*
three months I will conduct _____ *per month, which is*
approximately _____ *per week.*

To go one step further, you could also determine how many calls and contacts you would need to make in order to set up one Complimentary Coaching Session.

Of course when you first start out defining how many Complimentary Coaching Sessions you need to conduct to close on one new client, it can be difficult because you don't have a closing ratio yet. However, you could just guess until you know your closing ratio.

GENERATING PASSIVE COACHING INCOME

WHAT IS PASSIVE COACHING INCOME

Passive income is income you generate from something you created such as an e-book, e-course, a hard cover book, distance learning course, or digital products such as CDs, MP3s, or DVDs. The benefit of creating products to generate passive income is that you only have to put in the effort of creating the product once but you can enjoy the rewards of your effort over and over again. Generating passive income is the easiest way to earn income because you don't have to work to earn money; all you have to do is work hard once to create it.

Multiple streams of income

As a coach you have the potential to generate multiple streams of income. Generating income from coaching engagement is great; however, you want to have multiple streams on income to set yourself apart from having to work in order to earn income. Think about it, if you would get sick, or you want to take a longer vacation, during that time, you would not earn a dime because you are not producing income.

If you would have multiple steams of income however, you would still earn income because you have systems in place such as selling your products online or have affiliates selling your products for you. If you only coach clients one-on-one, eventually you reach your capacity because you can only coach a limited about of clients. Therefore, your income will be limited.

As a coach you can leverage your knowledge by saving everything you say, write, or create and use all this material to create your own products. You have three types of passive income strategies which are truly passive, leveraged and residual.

Truly passive income would be any products you create such as e-books, e-courses, audio programs, or manuals. Reason why they are considered truly passive is because once you have established these products you have nothing else to do other than market them through the same strategies you are already marketing your coaching business.

Leverage income are products created from existing content you have created in the past such as emails to clients giving tips or explaining how to do something a certain way, blog posts, newsletter content, or any other content you had already created. You would simply use your existing content to create a product such as a workshop, or e-books, etc. Basically, you don't have to recreate the entire content for your product; instead you leverage your existing content.

Residual income relates to membership-based coaching programs, subscription web site, or reseller commission such as affiliate program. This type of income is possibly the most lucrative type of income you can generate, but it may take some time to establish.

As you can see, as a coach you have multiple ways to generate income besides from coaching engagements. You should consider having a combination of all three income strategies to create predictable sources of income from your coaching business.

CREATING YOUR FIRST PRODUCT

If you are reluctant to creating your own products, let me tell you, it is the best way to position yourself as an expert, it provides credibility, it helps pre-qualifying coaching prospects, and most of all, it offers possibilities of multiple streams of income. If you are concerned about how much time and effort it takes to create your own products, let me assure you, it is not as bad as you might think. I honestly never thought I would be writing my very own book or creating my very own workshop, but I did! Certainly it does take time and effort but I am telling you, once you have created your own product and see the results you are getting and the satisfaction from accomplishing and creating something that will make a difference in someone's life, all the hard work and time spend doing research and typing away, was well worth it. Let's face it, it might take you a month to write a book or to create an e-course but you will create income for a very long time.

As a matter of fact, every successful coach offers a series of different products such as books, e-books, e-courses, manuals, workshops, seminars... you name it. Many offer their products in a bundle or separately. They offer their products during workshops, seminars, other speaking engagements, on their website, and through affiliates.

If you are just starting out creating your very first product might seem like a dreadful thing to do. However, it is not as difficult as it might seem. As you don't have a full coaching practice yet, you still have time on your hand to dedicate to creating a product. Having a product to showcase will also help you get new clients because like I mentioned earlier, it gives you credibility. As you are about to see there are different options you can choose from to create a product that will allow you to position yourself as an expert and that will help you get more qualified clients.

E-Books vs. Book

I am sure you are familiar with what e-books are; they are books in digital format. An e-book doesn't have to be long; it can even be as short as ten pages or as long as you want. Offering e-books is a great way to generate passive income because you can place it on your website or post it in different places online and people can buy your e-book any time they want. If you are wondering why writing an e-book would be beneficial, I will tell you why.

First and foremost, people want information fast, and an e-book gives them just that because there is not long waiting period to receive the e-book once it was purchased because it is digital and buyers get immediate access to the information. It also provides instant gratification. E-books are also a great way of displaying your expertise and knowledge and there are many people who want to know what you know, and they are willing to pay for it.

Writing e-books can be relatively convenient because you don't have to deal with publishers and they are relatively easy and quickly put together, whereas if you decide to write a book, the process takes much longer. Offering an e-book on a specific topic you coach people on would also be a great solution for those who can't afford your coaching fees.

What you could do is offer your e-book to those who would like to make a change in their life but your coaching fees are not feasible at that time or they would like to get a taste of what you know first before they decide to hire you as their coach. E-books are usually not very high in price so even those who can't afford your coaching would at least be able to purchase your e-book.

Many coaches also give their E-Books away for free and as a form of lead generation strategy. You could offer a short E-Book on your website as a Free Product in return for the individuals contact information or email address. If you decide to give your E-Book away for free I would suggest making it a short E-Book of ten to fifteen pages. If you have a larger E-Book you could make a shorter version as an introduction and give the introduction away for free with a call to action at the end of the free E-Book, to purchase the complete E-Book.

The satisfaction that comes with writing and publishing your very own book is unbelievable. Now-a-days, you do not have to be a professional author to publish a book, anyone can write a book. All you need is the desire to write and to share your knowledge with others. With the help of Amazon you can publish your book relatively quickly and easy. If this is of interest to you, there are books available where you can learn about how to publish your book on Amazon Kindle and how to use Publishers such as Create Space or Book Baby to get our book publishes as a Hard Copy.

How to write an e-book or a book

First you should brainstorm different topics you would like to write about and which are relevant to your target market. Think of specific problems they are having and make your e-book the solution for their problem. You could even do a survey where you ask different people specific questions as to what troubles and problems they are facing in that particular area.

Once you have a good idea of what you want to write about, select a topic that is appealing to your audience; "How To" topics usually sell best. Next, make an outline of your e-book, make note of what you will be covering in your e-book and also in what order.

Next you would create your cover. Find someone who can create a professional looking cover for you or do it yourself if you are familiar with graphic design. Creating your cover prior to start writing is also a great way to get you motivated to actually start writing. Once you created your cover, print it out and hang it on the wall by your desk or put it somewhere where you can see it this will get you motivated to sit down and start writing.

Now it's time to start writing! When you start writing, don't worry too much about grammar, the point here is to get your ideas out. Focus on writing valuable content. Write only a few pages at a time because you don't want to overwhelm yourself. Once you have written everything, you start editing and proofreading your work. Ask people you know and trust to read over your work or you can pay a professional to edit your work as well.

Once your content is written and edited and you have your cover and title, you decide on how much you will charge. Keep in mind, the price you set initially can be changed at a later time. Next convert your e-book into a PDF, HTML, EXE or whichever format is required from the publisher. If you upload your E-Book to your website I would suggest converting it into PDF for easy download after purchase. You also need to add your E-Book to your online shopping cart program on your website.

***

If you get stuck and you simply can't figure out how to get started or you suffer from "writers block" one exercise that can help you get your mind into creativity mode is to just start writing about anything that comes to mind. It doesn't matter what you are writing as long as you write. During this exercise you also would not worry about punctuation or sentence structure, or if it sounds good. Simply just start writing what comes to mind, even if it doesn't make any sense at all, it doesn't matter. The only thing that matters, you kick start your creativity. What I usually do is I start writing whatever comes to mind. Then I start writing about, wanting to start writing about whatever topic I am writing about and I slowly get my mind to think about that particular topic I am writing about. Not long after, I am so focused and concentrated on my topic and I can start writing.

E-Courses

An E-Course or E-Workshop is also a great way to generate passive income and can be created relatively easy and quickly, without a lot of technical knowledge required. E-Courses are completely automated where someone can purchase your E-Course and work on it on their own time, anytime they want, and they can start the course as soon as they purchase was completed. You can choose to send the course materials all at once after purchase or you can offer a membership site on your website that has the entire course on the membership site. An example for such E-Course can be found on my website **www.embracingsales.com/SalesAcceleration**.

Once someone purchases my E-Course they are redirected to create their member account to access the training material.

How to write an E-Course

The process of writing an E-Course is similar to writing an E-Book. You first start brainstorming a few topics relevant to your target audience and specific problems they experiencing and make your course the solution to their problem. Here again, you can conduct a survey were you ask different individuals about their problems and struggles to help you come up with different solutions to their problem. Once you decided on the topic, map out the entire course and make an outline.

Next choose the topic you want your E-Course to be about and decide on a title for example: "Learn how to increase your sales results in 10 easy steps". How-to topics are always good titles because people want to learn how to do something to fix their problem.

Once you have your title, now you create the content for your e-course. Depending on how you want to deliver your course, if it's through audio or video modules, or only in writing, you would create your content according to how you want to deliver your course. If you decide to do audio modules, you would create the different scripts for each audio module, practice the script and record it with an audio application such as Audacity for example. Audacity is Free and easy to use to edit and convert your audio.

If you choose to do video modules, you also would create the scripts for each module, practice your scripts and do the recordings. To edit your videos you could use a video editing application such as Video Studio Pro which is relatively inexpensive or you could choose a more expensive application such as Camtasia Studio, or Adobe Premier Pro.

If you decide to deliver your course in written format you would simply write all the content, edit it and convert the file into either PDF or HTML. PDF is a good option to allow users to download the modules or entire course and HTML would be for displaying the content on your website without the option of downloading the different modules. What you can do is to have the content for each module displaying on your website as HTML and offer the entire course as downloadable version.

Once you created your content, you would decide on how much you are going to charge for the course, as well as a sales page for your website. A sales page is a page that displays your course and should sound catchy enough to lead individuals to make a buying decision to purchase your course. You can either write the content yourself or you can find a copyeditor to write the content for you.

Next step is to upload everything to your website and create your sales page, add the course to your shopping cart program, create the membership option if applicable and start advertising.

If you decide not to offer the content of the course on your website to download or on a membership page, you could also set up an Auto responder message to send the entire course in one message or spread out over different days or weeks.

Create a Workbook

If you would rather not write a lot or create digital content, you could simply create a workbook with different activities, templates, and exercises to help individuals complete a specific task or to help them achieve a specific goal. Workshops are relatively easy to create and don't require a whole lot of writing other than explaining the different activities and exercises. You could also offer a workbook with your e-course or you could create an e-course accompanying the workbook at a later time.

TIME MANAGEMENT

Time Management is a vital part of any business, if your time management system is not effective you as a coach will not be effective in building your coaching business. I would not consider myself a time management expert; however, I practice proper time management on a daily basis. Proper time management is simply about making the right *time choices*. The better time choices you make and the better you plan out your day, the more successful you will become. Many coaches and people in general, are experts in procrastinating. They come up will all kind of excuses why they can't make calls to clients, or why they can't do the things they need to do in order to build their business, or reach their goals. They spend their time with things that are not productive and then complain because they didn't get things done in time or at all. This is why it is so important to implement the proper time management system which will help you stay focus and get things done.

I am certain there are many different time management techniques available but today I will explain to you the time management system I use for myself. Feel free to use my system for yourself or share it with others who can benefit from a time management system as well. This system doesn't require a lot of time to learn or to implement, all it requires is for you to take fifteen minutes out of your day to complete your plan for the day.

To plan your day, I encourage you to either get up fifteen minutes earlier in the morning or do it right before you go to bed, it really doesn't matter when you do it, as long as you write your plan on paper. During those fifteen minutes of planning your day, ask yourself specific questions how to best plan your day. Such questions could be:

1. What are my goals today?

2. What is my commitment level for today?

3. How will I reach for success today?

4. How many calls do I need?

5. How many sessions do I have scheduled?

6. What new prospects will I call?

7. How will I improve my health today?

8. How much time will I spend with my kids/spouse?

9. What activities will I do with my kids/spouse?

10. What are my carry over activities from yesterday?

11. How much training will I be doing today?

12. What are my two most valuable outcomes for today?

13. How will I make this day count?

Start answering this list of questions and feel free to add to replace some of the questions to make the fit your needs. The point here is to have your own set of customized list of questions to help you plan an optimal day. When you sit down to plan your day, do so in a quiet area with no disruptions to get the most out of planning your day.

After you have answered the questions prioritize them and look at each task from the point of view of which activity, once completed, will provide the most value. Apply the 80/20 rule where the top twenty percent will provide, once completed, the most value and the bottom eighty the least amount of value. By defining the twenty percent activities on your list, you will feel less discouraged if you were unable to complete everything on your list. By focusing on the top twenty it will give you greater satisfaction because it gave you the most value.

PART III – THE SALES PROCESS - SELLING YOUR SERVICE

INTRODUCTION TO SELLING

You probably wonder: "Why do I need to know how to sell, I'm a coach not a sales person?" You see, technically you are a sales person because you do want to get prospects to hire you as their coach, right? In order to find prospects and get them to hire you as their coach, you need to know how to sell your service. Most people automatically resist when people try to sell them something and if you don't know how to properly talk to prospects, you will have a hard time trying to fill your coaching practice.

When I first started in the coaching business back in 2012, I did not know anything about sales and marketing to get clients, which caused me to not find or get any. It was not until I got so frustrated because I was not very successful in the network marketing business as I was in at that time or my coaching business; that I decided to be professionally trained in sales.

I am telling you from personal experience that in order to become successful in your coaching business, you must know how to sell, what to say to clients, how to set appointments, how to build trust and rapport, how to handle their objections and most of all how to close the sale. These are all skills you must have in order to be successful. However, the good part about this is, selling is a learned skill and you can learn how to close sale after sale with confidence and ease.

I am sure you know that there are many successful coaches out there that make six figure incomes but did you ever ask yourself, how they were able to become this successful? Before we get into this I would like to share with you something I have learned which can answer this question for you, it's about the 80/20 rule or also known as the Pareto principle. It basically means that the top 20 percent of all salespeople or in this case, coaches, earn 80 percent of the money and the bottom 80 percent only earn 20 percent of the money.

You see, those who made it into the top 20 percent, won't ever have to worry about not earning enough money or not having enough clients to keep their business going ever again but the bottom 80 percent, they barely make it and always worry about not having enough money coming in, and always worry about possibly having to get a regular full time job again because their income doesn't cover all their expenses.

Every year, many start their own coaching business with the hope of becoming successful, being able to walk away from their fulltime job and having the freedom of being their own boss. However, as many who start the coaching business, many also quit their coaching business because they were not able to build a profitable business. Let me ask you this, how do you think the most effective coaches were able to become that successful? They were professionally trained, they went to seminars not only to learn and improve their coaching skills but also to learn and improve their selling skills. They even had their own coach or trainer that held them accountable and pushed them to do better.

THE ART AND SCIENCE TO INCREASING YOUR SALES RESULTS

In order to increase your sales results and grow your business there are three fundamental parts that are very important. These components are generating leads, setting appointments and converting those leads. The lead generation component is all about getting enough leads or contacts with people who are in your target market and who would benefit, or are interested in hiring you as their coach.

The appointment creates the opportunity to present your coaching service to individuals who are interested in obtaining coaching services. Once you set the appointment you converted the leads into prospects and you have the opportunity to present your service to them and attempt to close the sale, or get the prospect to hire you as their coach.

The art and science of increasing your sales results not only includes the fundamental parts but also three important methods you should get to know. These ways are the inner game of selling which is the mental side of selling, your beliefs, your attitude, your comfort zone, and how you prepare yourself for presentations or coaching calls, and it is also how you handle objections on an emotional stand point.

There is also the outer game of selling which has to do with methods for selling your coaching services, it's the systems that you have in place, your database to track and store all of your contacts, it's the steps of the sales process, and it's also the three fundamental parts to grow your business. It includes the way you talk to your prospects, how you close the sale, the scripts you use, and how you follow up.

The last part of increasing your sales results is taking action; it's following through and doing what you know you should be doing in your business. It's the goals you set, the way you manage your time, it's the number of calls you make on a daily/weekly basis, and it is also your level of commitment. Without taking action the first two elements wouldn't even matter because only those who take massive action and work towards reaching their goals and dreams, only those will become successful.

BELIEFS, MINDSET AND OVERCOMING LIMITING BELIEFS

One big obstacle many coaches face is their mindset about selling or asking prospects for the sale. That is totally understandable because many have a fear of rejection or being told no. Even though this is an understandable fear, it is holding you back and causing you to resist selling. Even your clients have a resistance to sales people because first of all, it's our society or culture that trains us to resist sales people, and secondly, no one likes to be sold on something. Your resistance to selling or negative feelings around selling however; reflects in every presentation you give, in every call you make, and every time you try to close a sale.

What I am about to share with you might help you shift your mindset around selling and possibly could help you to embrace selling instead of resisting selling. Instead of focusing on making a sale, focus on providing service and value, sell out of honesty and compassion for your clients, and instead of pushing your clients into hiring you as their coach, lead them and guide them to make a decision that you can truly help them and transform their life. This is one thing I find that most sales people and coaches are lacking; they focus more on closing the sale rather than providing value.

If you truly focus on providing value and that you honestly care about the prospect or client, you should not have to fear selling or asking for the sale. Remember the section about the law of beliefs and the mindset in Part I of this book? The same principle applies to the mindset about selling. If you feel you have a resistance to selling, you can use positive affirmations to reprogram your subconscious mind to eliminate your limiting beliefs about selling, or asking for the order.

THE SALES PROCESS

The sales process is the heart of selling, it starts with generating leads, and then setting appointments, next is building instant trust and rapport with prospects, identifying their needs for your coaching services, closing the sale, handling the objections, and last but not least following up with those who did not acquire your services.

There are two key things I want you to understand about the sales process. The first thing is sequence. It's not only the words you say but also the sequence the words go in. For example, if you meet someone that you find would be a perfect candidate for your coaching services you would not just blurt out, "hire me as your coach, I am exactly what you need to fix your problem." No, there is a process you have to follow before you can attempt to close. You have to sell your clients "up the selling ladder" and you do that by following the sequence of the sales process.

The second thing I want you to understand about the sales process is that you can work on each step by itself. What I mean by that is, if you are good in one step for example, generating leads, but you could improve your building trust and rapport skills than you can focus on that one step until you get better and feel more comfortable with building that instant trust and rapport with prospects or your clients. Once you feel comfortable with building trust and rapport you can move on to the next step that you want to improve.

By dissecting the sales process and focus on each step by itself it makes it less overwhelming. However, if you learn the steps of the sales process and follow its sequence it will not only increase your sales results but possibly even give you the breakthrough that you have been waiting for.

I. *Generating Leads*

Generating leads has one simple purpose; to generate a lead. During the lead generation process you would not give a presentation, or close, you simply want to get leads. Look at lead generation as a stand-alone process or activity in the sales process. What that means is if for example you go to a networking event and meet someone interesting or someone you think is in your target market, you wouldn't try to sell them your coaching services right there and then, instead you ask for their business card or contact information.

One mistake I see other coaches make is that they are explaining their coaching program when they meet a potential client for the first time. By doing too much too soon it creates a repelling energy and the prospect will less likely to buy from you.

Instead of trying to pitch your sales presentation as soon as you meet someone, get their contact information and plug their information into your database. The lead generation process is simply to get leads and to add them to your database of prospects.

Database

A database is a critical aspect of your business and necessary to manage your leads. The best way to keep track and manage all of your leads and contacts is to enter them into either a spreadsheet program like Excel or a Customer Relationship Management (CRM) software application such as Less Annoying CRM, Insightly, Constant Contact or Zoho just to name a few. Enter each contact as well as any other important information that would be beneficial to you.

Lead Inventory and setting a lead generation goal

In order to build your lead inventory you must first input all of your contacts into your database. Once you entered all of your contacts into your database you now have your lead inventory. To expand your lead inventory I strongly suggest that you develop a lead generating goal. If you are wondering why you should set a lead generating goal, it is because a goal is like a magnet; once you set a goal you will attract the key elements needed to accomplish that goal.

Your goal should be to develop a set number of leads that you will add consistently to your database within a set period of time. For example, my goal is to add 25 new leads to my database each month. You could also develop a weekly goal of generating let's say five leads a week.

You might even have daily goals or a series of goals but the most important part to remember about setting goals is to write them down and to refer to your goals on a regular basis. Also, keep track of your goals, measure, and review your results to determine if your goal was set too high or not high enough. If that's the case, refine your goals.

When first starting out, the best thing, and this is what I tell my clients, is to get a list of 200 leads as soon as possible and to start prospecting to them to introduce their coaching business. I know you probably wonder: "How am I supposed to get 200 leads?" No worries, I am about to share with you different lead generation techniques that will help you.

Multiple Lead Generation Systems

The key to successful lead generation is to have multiple lead generation systems in place. I am about to share with you a few lead generation techniques that you could implement relatively quickly.

Asking for Business Cards

The easiest way to get a lead is by simply asking. When you meet someone that you find is in your target market and would like to prospect to, you could simply ask: "Would you like to exchange business cards?" It's that simple and works almost all of the time. If they don't have a business card you could simply say: "Could I get your contact information? I would love to stay in touch. "They can scribble their information on a piece of paper or in today's time and age, you could enter it into your cell phone that way you won't risk losing the piece of paper.

Go where you spend your money

The next lead generation idea is go where you spend your money. Now this might not work for everybody, depending on what type of coaching business you're in. Simply think about the people that you pay money to on a monthly basis; are any of them in your target market? If so, enter their names and information into your database and start prospecting to them.

Think about it, anyone that you pay money to, for example your hair stylist, those who work at your favorite supermarket, those who fix your car, do your landscaping, your drycleaner, your dentist or chiropractor, just think about all the different places and people you pay money to. You already have a relationship with them and that rapport.

Think of all the places you pay money to and ask yourself: "Are those people in my target market?" You probably have at least 10 to 20 people that you pay money to, maybe even more. I would suggest make a list and add everyone that you can think of where you spend your money and enter their information into your database and start marketing to them.

Person of Influence

The next strategy I want to share with you is the Person of Influence strategy, also considered forming a Strategic Alliance. A Person of Influence is a person who has your target market in their network. Everyone has a network but not everyone is a Person of Influence. Make a list of 10 people that you would like to develop a relationship with, a person that has your target market in their network.

It should be someone who has a high percentage of your target market; you may or may not even know them. Call them up and ask if they would like to meet to discuss how the both of you could build a relationship through collaboration. What that means is that the Person of Influence will refer his network to you and you will refer your network to them. When meeting with the Person of Influence, look for ways to add value to each other's network, and develop a plan.

Raffle Bucket

The Raffle Bucket technique is a good way to get a lot of contacts or leads relatively quickly without too much effort on your part. Have you ever been to a networking event where they held a raffle and in order to participate, everyone had to drop their business card into a bucket or bowl? The reason why they asked for business cards is not only because it makes it easier to call out the name of the person who won the raffle but it is also a great way of collecting leads.

Think about it, let's say 100 people are at the event and they all dropped their business card into that fish bowl, the host now has 100 qualified leads to contact after the event. However, sometimes you get a host that doesn't consider the value that is in that fish bowl. So the next time you go to such an event don't focus on winning the prize, instead focus on the value of the fish bowl and if the host doesn't seem to see the value, go and ask if you can have the bowl of business cards.

Referrals

Referrals are one of the best leads you can get, because it is very predictable as far as the results in most cases. If you don't ask for referrals, you are potentially leaving a huge amount of money on the table. One exercise you could do is, identify the financial value of a quality referral and then think about the lifetime value. What I mean by lifetime value is let's say you get one referral which has a financial value of $25 now think about it if that one referral turns into a long time client of yours, how much do you think would you earn from that one client?

Now, let me share with you a referral system that I personally use to generate a good number of referrals. Feel free to use this referral system to help you to consistently generate leads. A referral system is something you could implement right away, and I guarantee that you will get referrals. So having said that, think about any existing clients, do you think that they know at least four people and do you think that it is possible that they would meet at least three to four new people every three months?

Let me give you a referral system that you can consistently use to generate four referrals every three months from the same person. So it starts with a form that you can download from http://bit.ly/Referral-Form. Simply change the form to reflect your information.

Here is how it works, at the top of the form is a place where they would put their name, and below that the two boxes are called memory joggers, it helps them jog their memory of people. Then there are four squares there for the four referrals, and then there is the information on how they can get the form back to you. However, I have to let my client know what a good referral is for me, so here is a script on how to do this and feel free to use this script for yourself.

"Hello Mr. or Mrs. Prospect, I am planning on being in the coaching business for the next 20 to 30 years and I would love to receive referrals from you from time to time…… as a matter of fact I would like to ask you for a few referrals right now if that's ok with you. To help you with this, let me explain to you what a good referral is for me….. I look for male or females between the age of 20 and 55 who are not very satisfied with their life, who would like to lose weight, make positive changes in their life, or who would want to life a less stressful and more fulfilling life
.(change this to reflect your coaching services).

When you think of a good person for me, think about any active or retired military from any branch of service, friends, family, coworkers, neighbors, acquaintances, past employers, workaholics, network marketers, sales people, anyone that you know that would benefit from making positive changes in their life.

Now, off the top of your head, can you think of at least four people? While you are thinking about that, let me give you an incentive, each one of these boxes on that form is worth $25 dollars. That's right; if they check out and they are qualified I will give you $25 for each referral. Now I always tell clients, hold on to the form until you have four referrals because that makes it easier for me to just send you a one hundred dollar bill. So how does that sound for an incentive?"

This is a great strategy to consistently get referrals but be advised, if you are just starting out or don't generate enough income to offer $25 per referral you can lower the amount to $10 or even $5 or you could offer something else that is of value.

Offer something for FREE

Another great strategy is to give something away from free in exchange of receiving someone's contact information. Something free could be a free report or article, or a short audio or video, something of value to the prospect. You could use something called a Squeeze Page, which is a small web site with the sole purpose of getting someone to enter his or her information in exchange for a free item. You could also add a sign up form on your website with the same purpose of giving away something for free in exchange for their information. On my website for example I offer different free reports in exchange for the users contact information. Once someone requested any of the free reports, their contact information goes straight into my database. I now have a lead.

The best part about it is it tells me what topics they are interested in. For example if someone requests the report on "How To Improve Your Emotional And Mental Health," I now know that they could benefit from my Holistic Life Coaching services.

Recycled Leads

Did you know that you can recycle leads? You could call a lead every 90 days and offer them the same offer until they either say yes or tell you to stop calling them. I'm not saying you should recycle your leads, especially if you don't feel comfortable with calling them multiple times but it is an option. Most of the time if you call them after 90 days, they don't even remember ever speaking with you before.

Public Speaking Engagements

Another great way of getting leads is through Public Speaking. This might not work for everyone but for those who feel comfortable speaking to a large group, public speaking might be the best lead generating strategy. If you are interested in public speaking but don't feel comfortable or you feel you lack the skills then you might want to consider joining a toast master group in your area. Toast Master groups teach their members how to properly give speeches.

Additional Ways of Generating Targeted Leads

Additionally you can generate leads through your website, through targeted traffic to your site. The best way to generate targeted traffic is by using services such as Google AdWords where you pay for clicks on specific keywords to your site. However, if you are just starting out, this might not be a good option for you because it can get pricey and you would also need SEO-Search Engine Optimization on your site which also usually requires you to pay someone to get it done right, unless you know SEO.

To get traffic to your site or targeted leads you can be active in forums, online groups, blogs, or online article sites, in your target area and provide value. One thing to remember when posting in forums or online groups is to provide more value than merely advertising your services. By providing value you show that you are an expert in your area and once you build a reputation of being an expert people will start connecting with you or reaching out to you.

This lead generation technique might be one of the slowest, but once you build your reputation it will be much easier to get leads that way.

II.   Setting Appointments

Appointment setting is a critical aspect of a successful sales career and you must develop the proper mind set about setting appointments in order to become successful. As I mentioned earlier there is the inner game, the outer game and action in regards to the sales process at a whole but it also applies to each of the steps individually. What that means is there is the inner game of appointment setting which includes your mindset about appointment setting. The outer game relates to how you set appointments as far as what you say, when you say it, and how you say it. Action relates to actually making it happen, making the calls and setting the appointments.

The first step is developing the proper mindset about appointment setting. Avoid thinking of appointment setting as a dreadful thing you know you have to do. Instead think of it as a fun and easy thing to do and if you get a no, don't take it personally because the prospect didn't say no to you, they simply said no to your offer. But keep in mind, the sole purpose of setting an appointment is simply to set an appointment. It's not to sell your coaching service. That's what the appointment is for but when you're setting the appointment, you should focus on just getting your foot in the door and making the appointment.

When setting appointments you have to sell the benefits of the appointment, but remember the benefits of the appointment are different than the benefits of your coaching service. That means, you have to provide the prospect with enough value, for them to decide to take time out of their day to meet with you.

Think of it as a teeter-totter; on one side is time and on the other side is value. In order for the prospect to agree to take valuable time out of their day to meet with you, you have to provide them with enough value so it will out weight the value of their time and make the teeter totter tip over. I'm sure you have had times when you tried to set appointments and the prospect just did not agree to set up an appointment with you. It is very likely that you may have not given them enough value to make them want to take time out of their day to listen to what you want to share with them.

Here, I will give you an example. Let's say I am calling up a potential client to offer a complimentary coaching session.

"Hello Mr. or Mrs. Prospect, my name is Kay Sander, I am a Sales Acceleration Coach who specializes in working with sales people and network marketers to increase their sales results. The reason for my call is that I would like to schedule a time with you for a free business check up or goal setting session. The session will be done via phone (that's a benefit) at a time that is convenient for you (that's a benefit) and I will assist you in clarifying your goals and visions, identify key strategic mile-stone objectives, uncover hidden challenges that could be sabotaging your success, and we will create a three stage plan and next step action plan (that's multiple benefits) that will allow you to increase your sales results. I'll answer all of your questions (that's another benefit).

At the end of our session, you will have the opportunity to hire me as your Coach and trusted mentor if you feel comfortable. How do you feel about setting up an appointment?"

I just shared the benefits of the appointment with the prospect now when we have our session; I will be going over the benefits of hiring me as their coach. But remember, the benefits of the appointment are different than the benefits of hiring me as their coach; it's a different kind of benefits but overall, that's what people want, they buy benefits. With that said, you must give enough benefits for the prospect to make a buying decision.

I suggest making a list of the key benefits the prospect gets from meeting with you, as well as the benefits of the benefits and the consequence of not meeting with you. There are different strategies you can apply when setting up appointments. One is reducing the risk. By reducing the risk the client is more likely to say yes. For example, if you were to reach out to one of your prospects or POIs wanting to set up a time to give a presentation to the people in their network but they don't feel comfortable setting up that appointment with you because they either don't know you or they don't know what you have to offer.

To reduce the risk, you could simply ask if you could come out and have a five-minute conversation with them to give them an overview of what it is you do, so he or she can meet you. By offering to meet just for a few minutes you get the opportunity to connect with them and build rapport. Once you build that connection and the prospect knows more about what it is you do, you will be more likely to close on setting up an appointment at that time.

Using pre-framing when setting up appointments allows you to let your prospect know in advance what's going to happen. For example you could say something like this:

*"Mr. or Mrs. Prospect, for me to best help you when we meet, I would like you to answer the following questions and email them to me prior to our session (*ask specific questions to get an understanding where they are at and what they want to accomplish according to the niche you are coaching). *Can you have these done and emailed to me prior to our session?"*

Prior to setting any appointments, I suggest you make sure to have all your necessary tools available to aid in the process. These include having an appointment setting script, a confirmation email, and an information email in case the prospect or client requests more information. Create objection response scripts to what to say when prospect has objections to setting up an appointment with you.

Make sure to have an inventory of leads to contact, have a calendar and block out specific times where you will make calls to set appointments. Most of all, track your results. It is important to track the number of calls you make on a daily basis, the number of conversations you had, the number of appointments you set, the number of voice mails you left.

Use appointment setting script

When you create your appointment setting script, keep in mind that your script has to get the prospects attention and the first 30 seconds when talking to someone are most important and define if the prospect is going to keep listening to you or if they are going to hang up or close the door on you. You must have a good and strong beginning to get their attention. Here is an example

"Mr. or Mrs. Prospect, my name is Kay Sander and I am a certified Holistic Life Coach. I was wondering if you would be interested in a proven method that can help you live a more fulfilling life, a life that can bring you everything your heart desires?"

Your opening statement must answer one simple question. Why the prospect should listen to you, and it should result in the prospect asking. What is it?

Focus solely on the key benefit but avoid high pressure. You could say something like: *"I only need 30 minutes of your time to show you what I have to offer and you can decide for yourself if it is the right thing for you."*

Or you could say: *"I just want to show you something that many of my other customers are using and they are very happy with the results they are getting. If you have 30 minutes I can show you what it could do for you and you can judge for yourself."*

Many times prospects try to ask questions to find out more about the product or service but don't answer any questions simply say: *"I know you must have a lot of questions but I will give you all the answers when we meet."* Or *"This is a very good question however, in order to provide you with the best value and to answer all of your questions it is best for me to show you when we meet."*

When you set up the time don't give the prospect too many choices. Offer them two time slots and if they are not available during either, ask what day would be best for them and offer them a specific time slot on that day. Selling is about leading and that also applies to setting appointments. One thing to remember, always confirm the appointment either the day prior or a few hours prior to the appointment or there is a strong possibility that you show up to the appointment but the prospect doesn't.

Ways to set appointments

There are different ways to set appointments; it does not necessarily have to be done by phone. You can set appointments via email, automated appointments through your website, during speeches, while at another appointment, via text message, through social media, or you could even pay someone to set appointments for you.

III. *Building instant trust and Rapport*

Building trust and rapport in the sales process is the most important part of selling. Why? Simply because people buy from people they like and trust. If a person doesn't like or trust you they won't hire you as their coach. You can give the best presentation or complimentary coaching session ever and end up with no one signing up for your coaching program. Why? It could be because you did not win the prospect's trust. Most prospects enter the presentation with the mindset that you are trying to get them to buy from you, and if they don't connect with you and trust that you want to help them with their problem, they will be less likely to buy. Even though your coaching service is exactly what they need to help them with their problem. Rapport focuses on creating a state of harmony with the clients. Rapport reduces resistance.

To create that instant rapport find common grounds, look for connections with your clients. For example, you both like to work out, or your children play on the same soccer team. Such similarities will help build that connection and instant rapport, because now you are no longer just a salesperson; instead, you are someone the client has something in common with. Being in the moment, listening to the client, and paying attention also build rapport. Genuinely care about the client, means caring more about the client and providing them with a solution for their problem than if you are going to make a sale or how much you will get out of the sale.

To gain a deeper level of rapport be present with your clients and view their experience and views from their perspective. In the book The Seven Habits of Highly Successful People by Stephen Covey, one of the habits is "First to understand, and then be understood." When you are with clients, nothing else matters, pay close attention to your client; it is all about them. If you have things going on that distract you, put them aside until after your meeting with your client. If you are not fully focused on them they will notice.

I am sure you know that most people already have a negative feeling about sales and sales people in general and you have to work even harder to overcome their resistance and negative feeling and show them that you don't just want them to hire you as their coach but that you truly care about them and that you have a solution for their problem. Care about your client more than you care about the outcome of your presentation or complimentary coaching session, which is your coaching fee.

Another effective way of building instant trust and rapport is by being humorous. Humor builds rapport. Try and incorporate humor into your presentation or initial session, or when you first call up prospective clients. As I mentioned before, the first 30 seconds when talking to someone are the most important 30 seconds where you not only have to get them interested but also build that instant trust and rapport.

IV. *Identifying the prospects' needs*

The purpose of identifying customer needs is to find a want, a need, or a problem that the prospect has that your coaching service can solve. The reason why we must do this is because a satisfied prospect or client does not buy and the easiest way to get someone to hire you as their coach is to find out what they want and desire and then give it to them. You might think your service is exactly what they need but the prospect might not feel that way. However, once you know what the prospect's true wants and needs are you can use that knowledge during your presentation or initial coaching session and make your coaching service irresistible. Many sales people and also coaches make THIS mistake. They skip the identifying customer needs section of the presentation.

I want you to think about recent coaching sessions you had with potential clients. How effectively did you identifying their true needs? Have you been taking the time to ask questions to find out what's most important to them and why they want to make a change? One mistake I see a lot of coaches make is they go straight into their coaching session and go over their pricing packages and there's a place for that; but before we go into the session and cover the features and benefits of your coaching service, you first want to find out what's important to this person and what their true needs and desires are. The way we find out what's important to them is by asking questions.

Here is a scripting idea that you could use when getting ready to ask the probing questions:

"For me to best help you Mr. Prospect I need to ask you a few questions. Would that be okay?" or

"For me to best help you I have created a list of questions to go over with you. Would it be okay if I went over these questions and took notes?"

Examples of probing questions and probing statements

- Are you familiar with what coaching is? (If no explain coaching)
- Have you ever worked with a coach before?
- What do you expect to get out of coaching?
- What is your biggest concern?
- What caused you to be interested in this complimentary coaching session?
- How do you think would coaching impact your life/business?
- Tell me about your situation.
- What is most important to you about _____?
- How quickly are you looking to move forward?
- What is your budget?
- What are you looking to accomplish long term from _____?

The key to finding customers' needs is through asking questions. Prior to your next complimentary or initial coaching session, create a list of question to ask the prospect to clearly identify their true needs. Think of the most powerful questions you could ask! Only when you take the time to identify a prospect's need prior to jumping into the main content of your initial coaching session and prior to explaining your different coaching packages, are you more likely to be able to focus on providing value to the prospect rather than focusing on winning or closing the sale. Probing questions will help you learn more about the prospect which in return will help you tremendously in growing your coaching practice.

V. *Sharing the benefits*

People don't just buy just because they want to spend money, No, they buy because the like they benefit they get from having a particular product or service. Remember this during your next initial enrollment session. Focus on the benefits your client will receive from working with you as their coach. However, don't focus on the benefits that you like about your service, instead focus on the benefits the prospect will like. This is why identifying the needs is so important because what you might think is a great benefit of your service, might not be the same for your prospect. When you focus on the benefits that are most important to your client, it will build value in your presentation or enrollment session. Do you remember the example of the teeter- tooter? It's the same with the benefits, the benefits or value of your services has to out weight the price. One thing to remember, when you give a presentation to a group of people, understand, each person has their own set of benefits that they are interested in.

Let's talk a little bit more about benefits. There are five different types of benefits: tangible benefits, intangible benefits, the benefits of moving forward, the consequences of not moving forward and the benefit of the benefit.

Tangible benefits are things such as saving or making money, reducing debt, increasing credit score, losing weight, and so on.

Intangible benefits include things like increased confidence; piece of mind, feeling more relaxed and so on. Even though intangible benefits are difficult to measure they are still very important.

The benefit of moving forward and the consequences of not moving forward are closely linked. For example, let's say you are a weight loss coach. The benefit of taking action is the individual who is overweight, would be less worried that something would happen to them due to being overweight, they will have more of a piece of mind if they lose weight and get healthier and most likely will live longer. But if he or she who is overweight does not sign up for the coaching services and does not lose the weight, he or she might get really sick which will put hardship and worries not only on themselves but also on their family.

A lot of times, the "benefit of the benefit" is the real reason why people buy. For example, you purchased this book because you wanted to learn the ins and outs of a profitable coaching business, which is the benefit of purchasing this book. The benefit of the benefit however is how is your life going to be different once you build a profitable coaching practice and you earn more income? What kind of car will you be driving due to having a successful coaching business? How will you feel when you are able to walk away from your regular job because your coaching business is booming? That's the real reason why you purchased the book and that's really what you want, to start your own coaching business and to become a successful coach with a profitable coaching practice.

To significantly increase your sales results you must identify the prospect's benefit of the benefit and incorporate those benefits into your presentation. The way to incorporate the benefits you can do so by letting your prospect "imagine" what it would look like or feel like. For example if you are a health and wellness coach you could say: *"just imagine how great you would feel when you fit in size seven pants"* or *"just imagine you go for a walk without feeling completely out of breath and tired afterwards."* Imagine is a powerful word and stimulates the subconscious mind.

To identify the benefit of your product or service you could go to your satisfied clients and ask them how they have benefited from your coaching service. Now, one great way of delivering a powerful and effective presentation or initial coaching session is if you tell success stories. One great way of sharing the benefits of your service is to incorporate stories. You would be surprised how powerful stories are. Why? The answer is simple: because nothing sells more effectively than success. By sharing success stories of your clients it movies people emotionally, it reduces resistance and increases rapport, and it acts as invisible selling.

Ask your satisfied clients if you can use their story and if you are just starting out and don't have any success stories to tell yet, you can use your own story or stories of individuals in general who benefited from coaching. You can even use stories from clients who chose not to hire you and now regret it.

VI. *Closing the sale*

Closing the sale is the most dreaded part of selling and many sales people and coaches simply don't feel comfortable asking for the order. But in reality closing is part of the sales process and is simply the last missing part of a well-delivered sales presentation or initial coaching session.

Closing is one of the most profitable sales skills to have and it can be very easy once you know how to close. The good thing about it is, once you know how to close you will have that skill for the rest of your life. It's just like learning how to ride a bike, once you learned it you won't ever forget; you might get out of practice if you don't get on the bike for a long time but you won't ever lose it completely. However, if you don't know how to close, it can be the most frustrating and intimidating part of sales.

The reason why the close is so difficult is two-fold; the buyer feels the fear of making a mistake or buying the wrong thing, paying too much, or being criticized by other people. Because of that buyers end up backing away and not purchasing after all.

The second reason is the sales person's fear of rejection. No one likes rejection or the prospect saying no. Each of us deep down inside, has that fear of being told no, a fear of being rejected. Because of that, we avoid situations where someone could tell us no. This is why many coaches either don't ask for the order or hurry through the close simply because they are trying to avoid possible rejections.

By the way, if you are struggling with the fear of getting a no, you are not alone. Every coach had to deal and overcome the fear of rejection at one point in their coaching career. Selling is a learned skill and so is closing. Once you improve your closing skills you will be closing successfully more regularly and you eventually will overcome the fear of getting a no. Simply focus on improving each step of the closing process to get you one step closer to a successful close.

The close also has three key parts: your mindset about closing, the way you handle objections, and taking action to close. Your mindset about closing refers to how you feel about asking for the order. The way you handle the objections refers to what you say to overcome these objections, and taking action is getting yourself to step up and consistently ask for the order. Most sales people subconsciously feel uncomfortable asking for money, which of course makes them hesitate to close. Clients can pick up on such negative feelings, which results in them hesitating to buy.

Other sales people on the other hand are extremely aggressive when it comes to closing which comes across as pushy and buyers don't like to be pushed. Instead of fearing the close or being pushy when closing, think of it as providing service. My mentor Eric Lofholm taught me that selling equals service; that selling comes from honesty, integrity and compassion, and that selling is about leading and moving people to action. If you approach selling with this mindset, then you have no reason to be afraid of selling or ashamed to ask for the money.

To make your close more compelling and effective, you must plan it, write it down word for word and practice it until you remember it. Never go into a presentation or initial coaching session not knowing exactly what you are going to say or exactly how you are going to close. In sales we call this "winging it" and winging it is never a good thing. True, you might wing it really well sometimes but only if you are well prepared will you be able to consistently close sale after sale after sale.

With that said, I want to encourage you to practice, practice and practice some more until you can deliver your close naturally without even thinking about it, consistently, and time after time. Consistency is the key to success and to achieve this kind of consistency you must incorporate sales scripting into your coaching business. Many sales people are reluctant to use sales scripting, they feel rehearsed or fake but if you practice your scripts it will not sound rehearsed or fake. It will make you sound like an expert, like you know what you are talking about. The good thing about using a sales script is that you can tweak it, to make it sound very compelling and make changes to it when you notice something that you say doesn't have the effect you want.

Let's take a look at how to write a closing script. First of all I want you to understand that the close follows a specific sequence. To craft an effective close it goes in the order of price, what is included, risk reducers such as discounts, guarantees, or warranties. Then there is a reward strengthener such as bonuses, urgency builder by offering incentive of signing up today and the consequences of not taking action, and last but not least the call to action which is asking for the order.

Once you ask for the order you be silent and wait for the prospect's response. Don't try to fill the awkward silence by rambling on about your product. I know it is uncomfortable sitting in silence waiting for the prospect to answer but trust me if you stay quiet the prospect will start feeling uncomfortable too To break the uncomfortable silence they either agree to hire you or give you an objection. But we will discuss how to handle objections in the next chapter.

Now let's talk about the different ways you can close. The first way of closing is by **pre-framing**. Pre-framing means you create a framework for the close early on in the presentation. For example you could say: *"I have two outcomes for my presentation, the first outcome is to share with you some great strategies on how to make more sales. The second outcome is to share with you how my ongoing coaching program works. But I will give you all the details about that at the end of our session."* By using a pre-framing close you already give the prospect an idea of what they can expect and that at the end you will ask for the order.

Next is the **trail close** where you get the prospect to agree that if you meet their expectations during the initial coaching session, they will agree to buy. For example, a coach in the health and wellness business could say: *"if I would give you the first session for free and second session at half price, would you like to sign up for my coaching program?"* Or a finance coach could say: *"if I can help you reduce your monthly payments and pay off your debt twice as fast, would you be interested in signing up for my coaching services?*

The assumption close is where you assume the prospect is going to buy. You would say something like: *"which credit card would you like to use today?"*

With the sign-up form close you would walk your prospect through the close by providing a sign up form and help them fill it out. You would use simple command words such as *"put your name and address here, put your credit card information there."*

If you want to emphasize the savings when mentioning the price you could use the contrast close where you stress the contrast between the price for the service and the benefits you are offering.

The hot button close is a very powerful closing technique. The hot button is the key benefit of your product or service that the prospect wants more than anything else. Once you discovered what their hot button is you keep pushing that button over and over again. Every time you mention that hot button, your prospect's desire to sign up for your coaching service increases. On the contrary, every time you talk about something that is not really important to your prospect, the desire to purchase decreases.

I just introduced you to a few different closing techniques. Pick the one you like best or feel most comfortable with and practice the close over and over and over again until you feel comfortable about the close.

VII. Handling objections

Handling objections is part of the sales process and remember this, there is no close without objections; objections usually indicate interest. If there are no objections there is also no sale. Instead of resisting or dreading objections, welcome them because objections are the stepping-stones that get you one step closer to a successful close. In order to become successful in your coaching business you must be able to comfortably overcome objections. It is not always easy but with practice you will become better and better.

Objections are simply reasons a prospect gives for not buying and most objections are not even true. The reason prospects give objections, even untrue objections, is because it's simply a habit of people not wanting to make a decision. Please note, when talking to prospects or clients never use the word objections, instead say concern.

When you are at the end of you presentation or initial coaching session, ask for the order and be silent. The prospect then has three options: either they say yes, no, or they give you an objection. If they say yes you complete the sign up process, if they say no then accept the no and move on. If they give you an objection, handle the objection with one of the techniques I am about to share with you.

Consider it as a form of negotiation. If you think about it, we have to handle objections every single day in all areas of life. If you have kids for example, how many times have you negotiated with your kids? They ask to stay up longer, you tell them *"No, not today because its school night,"* but they keep trying to negotiate to get maybe 30 minutes longer or 15 minutes longer. Sometimes you give in and sometimes you don't. Does that sound familiar?

The good thing with objection handling in the sales industry is that you can prepare. Any industry has seven to common objections. You can make a list of those common objections and craft responses for each one.

The most common objections are:

I need to think about it

I don't have the time

I don't have the money

I'm not interested

I'm already working with someone

I have already tried it and it didn't work

I need to talk it over with someone

Can you send me some information?

You can address objections in different ways such as with a story, a question, by solving the problem, by bringing out additional objections, with a script, before it comes up, by showing the benefit, by reducing the risk, by negotiating, with intuition or by asking the prospect what would need to happen in order for them to move forward.

Let's look at these more closely. Handing the objection with a story is the most powerful method because stories act as invisible selling tools. When the prospect gives you an objection you could say: *"you know that reminds me of one of my clients, he had the same concern but he decided to give it a try and he ended up loving the work we did and the results he received from our coaching session. He called me up a month later and thanked me for taking the time to introduce my coaching services to him and giving him the opportunity to try it out for himself."*

Handling the objection by solving the problem is also a great way to eliminate it. Let's say the prospect says they can't afford to hire a coach at this time you could say: *" I can appreciate that but let me ask you, if you had the money right now, would you like to get started?"* If they say yes you can say: *"great here is what I can do for you, I can offer you a free consultation where we will go over your sales strategies and we will come up with a strategy where you can increase your sales results relatively quickly. I recently met with a client and we came up with strategies that doubled his sales results within the first month. If I could help you increase your sales results, would that interest you?"*

You can also answer objections with a question. For example if the prospect says the price is too high you could ask: *"What exactly do you mean?"* or *"How much is too much?"* or *"Too high compared to what?"* Or if they say they don't have the time you could say, *"When will you have the time?"*

By bringing out additional objections you often times can reveal the true objection. This technique encourages the prospect to be honest with you. For example if the prospect starts with saying they don't have the money you could say: *"I appreciate you being honest with me but besides not having the money, I'm sure you have other concerns, would you mind sharing those other concerns with me?"*

You can also answer objections before they even come up, by addressing the key objections within your presentation.

Objections provide a great opportunity for you to share or demonstrate the benefits of your service. They also give a great opportunity to reduce the risks. It allows you make changes to your offer. For example if you are asking for a six-month commitment and the prospect says the price for the six-month coaching commitment is too expensive you could reduce the risk by saying: *"I understand. Perhaps we could start off with a three month commitment? Does that sound good?"* If they still say it's too much, offer them a month to month commitment.

You can change the deal by negotiating the terms. It is similar to reducing the risk but the difference is that we don't change the deal we simply change the terms. For example, *"if I give you a 5 percent discount will you move forward today?"*

By asking the prospect what would need to happen in order for them to move forward, they basically will give you the answer and you can act on it accordingly.

One method I find very interesting is the Feel, Felt, and Found method, which I learned from Brian Tracy. When the prospect gives you an objection you respond by saying: *"I understand how you feel. Many clients felt the same way as you do. But this is what they found...."*

Another great way to handle an objection is with the instant reverse close, which might leave your prospect speechless for a moment. If a prospect gives you an objection you simply say: *"Mr. or Mrs. Prospect, this is exactly why you should sign up for my coaching services."* By responding in that way your prospect will be completely baffled.

We just covered how to handle objections during the close but I am sure you have had instances when you had to deal with objections right at the initial contact. It happens when you call a lead and they say: *"I'm not interested or I don't have time for this."* The way you can handle this is one, you accept it and move on, or you could say something like *"Mr. or Mrs. Prospect this is exactly why you should take a few minutes to listen to what I have to offer."* Or you could say *"I didn't think you would be interested and that's exactly why I am calling you."* The prospect will be surprised to hear you say this and possibly be speechless for a moment, which will give you the time to say your introduction and possibly get their attention.

The best way to become comfortable with handling objections is to make a list of objections and practice responding to them. Ask a friend or family member if they would practice with you so you can improve your skills and you will fell less anxious when talking to prospects.

VIII. Following up

Prospects do not always sign up with you right away; sometimes they want to wait, or they want to discuss it with their spouse, maybe they say they don't have the money right now. What that really means is that it is often just a stall because you haven't shown enough value. Sometimes it could also have a legitimate purpose of the prospect wanting to wait. With that said, if the prospect does not buy from you, you MUST follow up with them at a later time.

The follow up is a very important step in the sales process. Most prospects do not make a buying decision right away usually it takes somewhere from four to six touches until someone makes a buying decision. The key point here is that you must make prospect follow ups a key part of your sales strategy and don't be afraid to follow up either. What is the worst thing that could possibly happen? The prospect saying, "No, I'm not interested!"

Remember this: ***Follow Up, Follow Up, Follow Up, Until They Buy Or Die***

Let me tell you a quick story. Many years ago, prior to me starting my career as a sales coach, I was in the network marketing business and since I did not know any better I never followed up with potential clients. When I initially spoke with them and they didn't buy right away, I never followed up with them, which of course resulted in me losing out on a lot of money. One person actually had told me months after my initial contact with them that if I would have followed up with them they would have purchased and even signed up because they really liked the product just didn't have the money at the time I had reached out to them.

The moral from the story is, always follow up with prospects. If they said no initially, you can follow up with them every 90 days with the same offer. Most of the time, they don't even remember who you are, or that they had spoken with you a few months ago. Unless the prospect tells you straight out that they are not interested and that you should stop calling them, you can continue to follow up with them.

Here are some key points to remember when following up with prospects or clients

1. When they tell you to call them back on Tuesday around 3p.m. don't call the day before or the day after or a week later. Instead, call them on Tuesday around 3p.m.

2. Always stay polite and maintain rapport even when leaving messages

3. If you constantly get their mail box don't leave negative messages instead be funny, say something like hey John, I've called you a

few times now and I have your name on my list, I can't take you off my list unless I hear back from you. Please call me to let me know if you would like to move forward.

4. Consider leaving different messages

Every once in a while someone you try to follow up with says something like: *"Why do you keep calling me? I thought by ignoring your calls you would get the hint that I'm not interested."* When something like this happens I suggest you say something like: *"My apology, the last time we spoke you shared with me that you were interested in my coaching services and I just wanted to follow up with you. However, if you are no longer interested I will take your name off my list and won't call you again."* Such encounters can be very uncomfortable but simply brush it off and leave it at that and don't take it personally.

When following up with prospects remember, you can follow up in different ways, it doesn't always have to be with a phone call. You could even follow up via email, text message, through social media sites, through someone else, or by doing a walk-in. If one way doesn't work, try a different way. If you feel anxious about following up it could be that you have developed a negative mindset about following up.

Let me ask you this, how do you feel about following up? If your answer is similar to: "I feel like I am being too pushy and I am bothering this person. If they are interested they will call me eventually. Or what if they get mad at me when I call them again?" All these negative thoughts will keep you from doing what is necessary. To get the right mind set about the follow up, think of it as its part of your job, I am simply being professional, I am providing value, my job is to lead my clients to action, they are still interested something probably just got in the way. This is the mindset of a successful sales person, they do not think negatively about following up with their potential clients.

However, one thing you need to remember if the prospect doesn't buy from you at the time of the presentation and you follow up with them you have to start over again and share the benefits of your coaching service to raise their interest and desire to sign up again. Remind them about the things they liked the most about working with you and you might want to check up on their needs for your service again because things may have changed from the last time you had spoken with them. Once you got them re-focused on what they were previously most interested in, you then can try to re-close the sale. The prospect most likely will have additional objections before agreeing to move forward. When they do, you simply handle the objections with the techniques you have learned.

TAKING ACTION

In the previous chapters of Part III you have learned all about the art and science of selling, you have learned how to generate leads, how to set appointments, how to identify someone's needs and how to share the benefits. You have learned how to handle objections and how to close. In this chapter I will cover the last missing piece to the puzzle, which is taking action.

All the things you have learned in the previous chapters really won't matter if you don't go out and take massive action. It is not just enough if you know what to do or what to say; you must also apply what you have learned and go out and do it. Most of all, you have to do it consistently, over and over and over again.

One thing I want you to remember about taking action, action is the number one key ingredient to all success and all achievements. Without taking action, nothing is possible. Only when you take massive action and go out and do what you know you should be doing to grow your business, will you achieve massive results.

The Baseline Method

The Baseline Method falls within taking action. One thing I want you to remember is that in order to increase your sales results and to build a successful coaching business you not only need to know how to coach but it is also about having systems in place to get you the clients you need to run and grow your coaching business. The Baseline Method is one of those methods that you can use in every single area of your life, so whether you are looking to elevate your relationship with your significant other, or better your health, whether its sales, business, or whatever it is that you want to improve on; the baseline method is one of the most important methods out there.

Every sales person or coach has a baseline in terms of the results they are producing on a daily basis. One of the ways we all measure our results is in terms of income earned. So let's just use that as an example. Let's just say you are bringing in $4,000 a month in revenue, so your baseline would be the $4,000. Your baseline would also be everything that you are doing to generate the $4,000. Your time management system, your goal setting system, the numbers of phone calls you make on a daily basis, the number of appointments you run in a month…. It's everything. Everything you are doing to produce your current results.

And the method is simply this: continue to do what you have been doing, because you are producing a positive result. And then what you want to do is, add to your baseline. The best thing you can do is work with a coach, a trainer or a mentor because if you are working with someone they can give you feedback on things that you could add to your baseline or, you can also subtract something from your baseline that's not working. Another thing a coach or mentor can help you with is they can help you modify and improve things you have in your baseline.

Now, ask yourself this question, what is one thing that you could add to your baseline that you currently are not doing but if you would add it to your baseline, it would produce a better result.

The Strategy Approach

Another concept I want to share with you is what I call the strategy approach. It relates to the number of leads, appointments, and sales you need to reach our sales target; it is basically your set of sales goals. Think of any successful sales coach, Anthony Robbins for example. He became successful because he had a set goal of how many appointments he wanted to run each week and each month, and he also had a set goal of how much he needed to earn to reach his sales target. Even today he and every other successful coach keeps their strategy approach of how many appointments they want to run and how much they want to earn.

Do you have a strategic approach? Do you have a set plan on how many leads you want to generate on a weekly basis, or how many appointment you want to run each week? If you don't have enough appointments set for the upcoming week, think about what can you do to generate more leads in order to set the appointments? Have a set goal of how many appointments you want to run each week and do what you know you need to do to reach that goal.

To help you with your sales goals it would be beneficial if you would have a strategic approach where you define how many appointments you want to run each week and how many calls you would need to make to set your target appointment goal, as well as how many leads you would need. To define your goal, consider these questions: How much do you want to earn in a single month? How many appointments can you run in a month?

The reason why the strategy approach is so important and an essential part to your success is because it helps in clearly defining your sales goals and it will help you stay on track.

RESOURCES

TimeTrade: online appointment scheduling service

      http://www.timetrade.com/

Less Anoying CRM: Customer Relationship Management

      http://www.timetrade.com/

Insightly: Customer Relationship Management

      https://www.insightly.com/

UrOneStop Desktop Publishing: Web and Graphic Designing Service

      http://www.uronestop.com

Audacity: Audio recording and editing software application

      http://audacity.sourceforge.net/

AnyMeeting: For conducting webinars and Web Conferencing

      http://anymeeting.com/

StartMeeting: for teleconferencing, screen sharing, international calling service. The free version is great for individual coaching clients; it also allows you to record the call. http://startmeeting.com/

Meet Up: to look for meetups in your area. http://www.meetup.com

WordPress: blogging platform but also used to create websites

      https://wordpress.org/

SBA: The Small Business Administration offers many great tools and information for entrepreneurs https://www.sba.com

SBA Business Plan Tool: A tool to create your business plan online

      https://www.sba.gov/tools/business-plan/1

Get Response: online forms creation tools, Autoresponder, Landing Page Creator http://www.getresponse.com

HostGator: Web hosting services http://hostgator.com/

GoDaddy: Web hosting services https://www.godaddy.com/

Vistaprint: for all your printing needs http://www.vistaprint.com

Video Studio Pro: Video editing software application
http://www.videostudiopro.com/en/products/default.html

Wordpress plugins:

PageBuilder by SiteOrigin, Social Media Plugin, Under Construction, WordPress SEO, PayPal Shopping Cart, WooCommerce, Groups WooCommerce, Groups, WP Affiliate

Paypal: to accept payments online and/or to send invoices to your clients
https://www.paypal.com

Bitly: to shorten your links https://bitly.com

Dropbox: online cloud storage https://www.dropbox.com/home

EzineArticles: online database where you can submit your articles to
http://ezinearticles.com

Toastmaster: a group for speakers and for those who would like to learn how to properly give speeches http://www.toastmasters.org

Elance: to hire freelancers http://elance.com

ICF International Coaching Federation: If you would like to learn more about the main body of coaching https://www.dropbox.com/home

Coachville: Website for coaching programs http://www.coachville.com

FINAL THOUGHTS

Did you choose to become a coach because you wanted to help other? Do you want to share your gift and knowledge with others? Make a difference in people's lives? Or did you perhaps choose to become a coach because of the possibilities of being financially independent or being your own boss?

No matter why you chose to become a coach, you chose a profession that can ultimately change your own life as well as the lives of your clients. You will experience personal and financial success and the success of your clients. But you will also experience difficulties and challenges that come with every business. There will be times when you want to give up because challenges and obstacles are getting in the way trying to blind you from seeing the potential and success that lies ahead of you. However, I am certain that you have the potential and the strength inside of you to make it past any obstacle and challenges that present themselves.

I have provided you with the knowledge I gained from being in business for myself, learning from my mentors, taking classes, reading many books, and through trial and error. Most books do not tell you everything you need to know, and even though I covered a lot in this book, it is up to you to take what you have learned and add on to your knowledge.

I don't claim to know everything but I shared with you the most important things you need to know to get your coaching business started and enough to build a professional and most of all, profitable coaching business.

You already know enough about success and how to achieve it. Now the only question is, are you ready to take massive action to really make this happen? As Napoleon Hill said, "Knowledge is not power, it only becomes power when it's organized into a plan of action!"

Success does not come easily and especially when you first start out it can be a difficult journey. Sometimes there were days where I almost gave up because it seemed almost impossible that after everything I have done already; my coaching business was still not as successful as I wanted it to be. Instead of giving up and feeling miserable about the time I spent on making phone calls, taking all this training, and spending so much money, I saw it as a learning curve because I now have more knowledge than I did before which eventually will pay off.. Everything takes time to develop.

If at any time you feel overwhelmed or want to call it quits, feel free to reach out to me. Too many coaches quit too soon because they are struggling or feel like they are stuck. I don't want you to be one of those coaches who gives up before experiencing success. You have the ability to become as successful as you want; all it takes is patience, and dedication.

To help you stay on track you should consider working with a coach or mentor, someone that can keep you on track, that keeps you motivated and that holds you accountable. We all need a little push from time to time, and some guidance when we are about to fall off track.

As a thank you for purchasing my book, I would like to offer you a Complimentary Coaching Session as well as a 25% off coupon for my Sales Acceleration Training Program, use coupon code: BooKboNus

To Your Successful Coaching Career
Kay R. Sanders

For more information about Kay Sanders, her coaching services, or to set up a Complimentary Coaching Consultation visit
http://www.kaysanders.com

Sales Acceleration Training Program
http://embracingsales.com/salesacceleration/

www.ingramcontent.com/pod-product-compliance
Lightning Source LLC
Chambersburg PA
CBHW051908170526
45168CB00001B/290